Eyewitness
ANCIENT CHINA

Harness ornaments, 7th–6th century B.C.

Sword and sheath, decorated with brass and tortoiseshell

Stucco head of a Bodhisattva, 8th–9th century

Sihu, or spike fiddle, and bow, 19th century

Carved lacquer boxes

Jade ear scoop
and various
bronze tweezers

Eyewitness
ANCIENT
CHINA

Written by
ARTHUR COTTERELL

Photographed by
ALAN HILLS & GEOFF BRIGHTLING

Pottery tomb
figures, 7th–8th
century

DK Publishing, Inc.

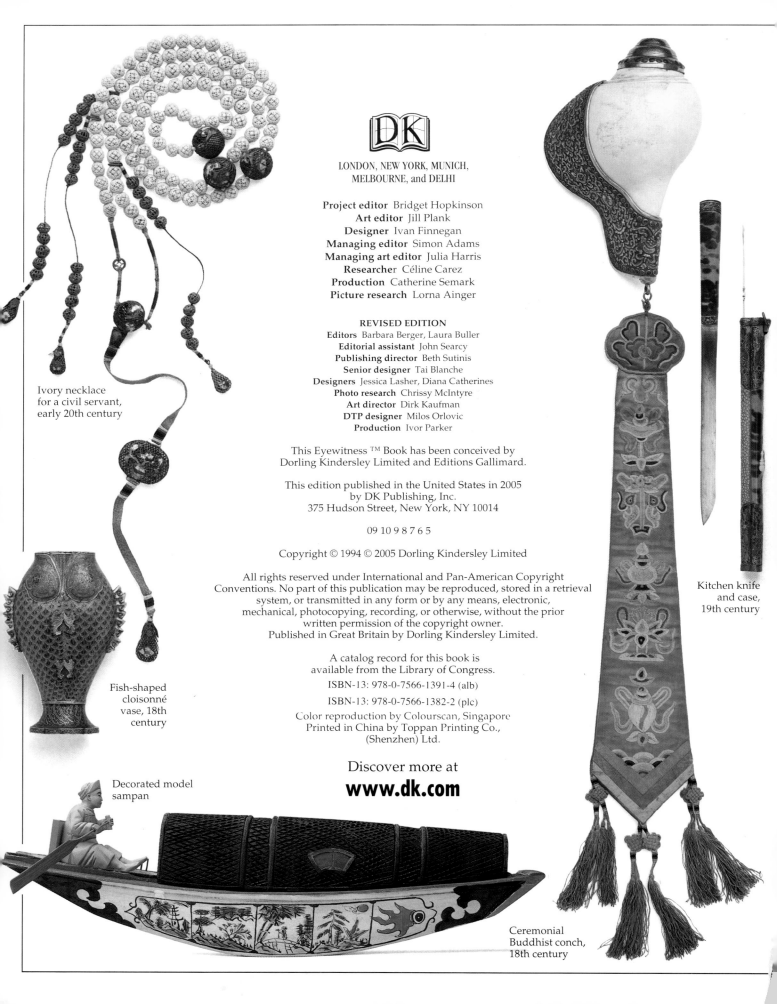

Ivory necklace
for a civil servant,
early 20th century

DK

LONDON, NEW YORK, MUNICH,
MELBOURNE, and DELHI

Project editor Bridget Hopkinson
Art editor Jill Plank
Designer Ivan Finnegan
Managing editor Simon Adams
Managing art editor Julia Harris
Researcher Céline Carez
Production Catherine Semark
Picture research Lorna Ainger

REVISED EDITION
Editors Barbara Berger, Laura Buller
Editorial assistant John Searcy
Publishing director Beth Sutinis
Senior designer Tai Blanche
Designers Jessica Lasher, Diana Catherines
Photo research Chrissy McIntyre
Art director Dirk Kaufman
DTP designer Milos Orlovic
Production Ivor Parker

This Eyewitness ™ Book has been conceived by
Dorling Kindersley Limited and Editions Gallimard.

This edition published in the United States in 2005
by DK Publishing, Inc.
375 Hudson Street, New York, NY 10014

09 10 9 8 7 6 5

Copyright © 1994 © 2005 Dorling Kindersley Limited

A catalog record for this book is
available from the Library of Congress.
ISBN-13: 978-0-7566-1391-4 (alb)
ISBN-13: 978-0-7566-1382-2 (plc)
Color reproduction by Colourscan, Singapore
Printed in China by Toppan Printing Co.,
(Shenzhen) Ltd.

Discover more at
www.dk.com

Fish-shaped
cloisonné
vase, 18th
century

Kitchen knife
and case,
19th century

Decorated model
sampan

Ceremonial
Buddhist conch,
18th century

Contents

Inlaid bronze
chariot decoration,
4th century B.C.

The world's oldest empire

CHINA IS THE WORLD'S OLDEST continuous civilization. From 221 B.C. to A.D. 1912, it was united under a single great empire. Ancient China remained untouched by outside influences because it was a world apart. Vast deserts and mountain ranges cut off China from other cultures in India, West Asia, and Europe, and many hundreds of years passed before the Chinese realized in 126 B.C. that other civilizations existed. China's social structure played a key role in maintaining its national stability. The civil service established by the first Han emperor helped successive dynasties govern the huge population wisely and effectively. Chinese philosophers also made a significant contribution to social harmony. Great thinkers such as Confucius encouraged people to lead an ordered, family-centered way of life.

CHINA UNITED
China was first united as a single state in 221 B.C. by the First Emperor. This map shows the boundaries of his empire. The Great Wall, seen at the top of the map, was built in about 214 B.C. and linked a series of older walls.

Bronze ritual water vessel, Zhou dynasty

Bronze ritual wine vessel, Shang dynasty

Bronze spearheads, Warring States period

Terra-cotta soldier, Qin dynasty

SHANG
China's first great dynasty was the Shang. This Bronze Age civilization is renowned for its skillful metalwork and for the emergence of the first Chinese writing. The Shang kings and their nobles ruled the mainly rural population from walled towns and cities. Horse-drawn chariots were the chief means of transport.

c. 1650–1027 B.C.

ZHOU
Confucius looked back on the early years of the Zhou dynasty as a golden age. The Zhou kings maintained the Shang practice of ancestor worship, and society was organized on a feudal system: great lords ruled the peasant farmers from large estates.

1027–256 B.C.

WARRING STATES PERIOD
As the Zhou declined, great lords fought each other for supremacy in what became known as the Warring States period. Vast armies clashed in large-scale battles and hundreds of thousands of men were killed. Confucius and other philosophers taught more peaceful ways of being, but their ideas were not adopted until later years.

481–221 B.C.

QIN
In 221 B.C. the First Emperor united China under the Qin dynasty. He built the Great Wall to protect his empire from the northern nomads, and standardized Chinese script, coins, weights, and measures. The First Emperor united China so firmly that afterward the Chinese people regarded imperial rule as the only form of government.

221–207 B.C.

Bronze mirror,
Han dynasty

Carved stone Buddha,
Tang dynasty

Ceramic water vessel,
period of disunity

Engraved silver dish,
Tang dynasty

HAN
The Han emperors consolidated the imperial system by establishing a national civil service. It was to run China for the next 2,000 years. Educated officials studied the teachings of Confucius and were selected by a rigorous examination system. State factories manufactured all kinds of goods, from iron plowshares to silk cloth.

207 B.C.–A.D. 220

PERIOD OF DISUNITY
In the period of disunity, China was divided into separate states, although it was briefly united under the Western Jin dynasty (265–316). Foreign peoples overran northern China, and in the south, various dynasties struggled for power. The gentle ideas of Buddhism first became popular in these years of unrest.

221–589

SUI
The Sui dynasty reunified northern and southern China. In their brief reign, the Sui emperors rebuilt the Great Wall and dug the Grand Canal. This great waterway linked the Yangzi and Yellow rivers, which improved communications and enabled grain and soldiers to be transported around the empire.

589–618

TANG
Under the Tang emperors, the Chinese empire expanded to become a great world power. This was a time of prosperity and cultural renaissance, in which both art and trade flourished. The civil service was reformed so that officials were recruited by merit rather than birth, and poetry was added to the examination syllabus.

618–906

7

Continued on next page

The empire continues

Although the Chinese empire experienced periods of unrest and disunity, and even conquests by foreign peoples, it existed as a strong state until modern times. China's borders ebbed and flowed with its changing dynasties, and the position of the imperial capital shifted several times, but the centralized government set up by the First Emperor survived for more than 2,000 years. There were many great innovations and technological advances throughout the empire's long history. The inventions of gunpowder, paper, printing, and industrial machinery all had an effect on Chinese culture. Nevertheless, the customs and traditions of the Chinese people, particularly those of the rural population, stayed remarkably constant.

Blue dish with a dragon motif, Song dynasty

Kublai Khan, the great Mongol ruler

Bronze flower vase, Song or Yuan dynasty

Blue and yellow glazed dish, Ming dynasty

Greenware dish, Yuan dynasty

FIVE DYNASTIES

In the Five Dynasties period, China was again briefly divided into north and south. A part of northern China fell under foreign rule, while the south was divided into numerous small states, many more than the name Five Dynasties implies. Southern China continued to prosper both culturally and economically.

907–960

SONG

China was united once more under the Song dynasty and reached its greatest heights of civilization. Advances in science and technology produced a minor industrial revolution, and the world's first mechanized industry was developed. Commodities such as iron and salt were produced on an industrial scale and were transported to distant parts of the empire on improved road and canal networks. The Song emperors were great patrons of the arts, and poetry, painting, and calligraphy reached new levels of perfection.

960–1279

YUAN

In the 13th century, China was conquered by the Mongols, who established their own dynasty, the Yuan. Throughout Mongol rule, Chinese scholars were banned from the civil service and many of them retired to write literature. Because the Mongols controlled the entire length of the Silk Road, international trade thrived. Many merchants became rich by exporting Chinese luxury goods. Marco Polo, and later other Europeans, visited China and reported on the marvels of its civilization.

1279–1368

Cloisonné ewer,
Ming dynasty

Delicately painted
porcelain dish,
Qing dynasty

CHINA TODAY
The map below shows the present-
day boundaries of China. It has
remained a strong world power.

Russia

Mongolia

Great Wall • Beijing

Yellow River Korea

Kaifeng

Xi'an • Luoyang

China Nanjing • • Shanghai

Hangzhou

Nepal

Bhutan

Bangladesh Taiwan

India

Burma • Hong Kong

Yangzi River

Thailand Laos Vietnam

MING
In less than a hundred years, the Chinese drove the
Mongols out of China and replaced them with the last
Chinese dynasty, the Ming. The Ming emperors set up
a new capital in Beijing, strengthened the Great Wall,
and improved the Grand Canal. They also extended
China's prestige by sending Admiral Zheng He on
great maritime expeditions to visit foreign rulers.
Chinese culture flourished once again, and the Ming
dynasty became famous for its exquisite arts
and crafts.

1368–1644

QING
The Chinese empire eventually collapsed under a
foreign dynasty, the Manchu, or Qing. The Qing
emperors lived in fear of a Chinese revolt and clung to
outdated traditions. For the first time, Chinese
technology fell behind other countries. Foreign powers
began to demand trade concessions and, after
a series of wars, China was forced to yield both
concessions and territory. In 1911, the Chinese
overthrew the weakened Qing government and formed
a republic. The Last Emperor stepped down in 1912.

1644–1912

AFTER THE EMPIRE
The Chinese republic, established
in 1912, lasted for only 37 years.
It was destroyed by war with
Japan and, after the Second World
War, civil conflict. In the civil war,
which lasted from 1946 to 1949,
Communist forces were victorious.
The Chinese Communist Party set
up the present-day People's
Republic of China in 1949.

1912– present

The beginning of China

THE FIRST CHINESE DYNASTY to leave a historical record was the Shang. The Shang kings ruled the greater part of northern China from about 1650 to 1027 B.C.; their heartland was the fertile land around the Yellow River. The Shang ruler was a kind of priest-king, known as the Son of Heaven. He was believed to be vested with all earthly powers and was expected to maintain good relations between the worldly and heavenly realms. The spirits of the royal ancestors were consulted for every important decision. The king alone possessed the authority to ask for their blessings, and he held the power to ward off ancestral ill will. Although the Shang rulers had many slaves, they relied upon the labor of their mainly rural population. The peasant farmers cultivated the land, took part in royal hunts, and served as foot soldiers in the army.

Jade *cong*,
c. 2500 B.C.

Jade ax head,
eastern China
c. 4500–2500 B.C.

PRE-SHANG JADES
These ancient jades were probably used in Neolithic rituals concerned with death. The *cong* may have represented the earthly powers.

A bronze blade was easy to cast and deadly on the battlefield

LETHAL WEAPON
The halberd, with a dagger-shaped blade, was a favorite weapon of war from Shang times onward. It was carried by foot soldiers and was also swung at the enemy from speeding chariots. Most fighting, however, took place on foot with spears and small knives.

The halberd was mounted horizontally and was swung like a scythe

Light brown jade with beautiful gray streaks

Ear or horn

Taotie, or monster face, a popular Shang motif

Eye

Mouth

HEAVENLY SPHERE
This jade disk is called a *bi*. Large numbers of *bi* have been found in Neolithic burial sites in China, along with *cong* and ax heads. These precious objects were laid along the limbs of the dead; the circular *bi* seems to have represented Heaven. Similar disks were used in the Shang dynasty. In Shang belief, the high god of Heaven, Shang Di, blessed the ruler with good harvests, victories on the battlefield, and strong sons. All important questions were referred to the spirits of the royal ancestors in the heavenly realm before decisions were made.

RITUAL CAULDRON
The Shang made offerings of food and drink to the spirits of their ancestors in special religious ceremonies. Food was prepared for the dead as if it were a banquet for the living. It was served to the ancestors in highly decorated bronze vessels like this *ding*.

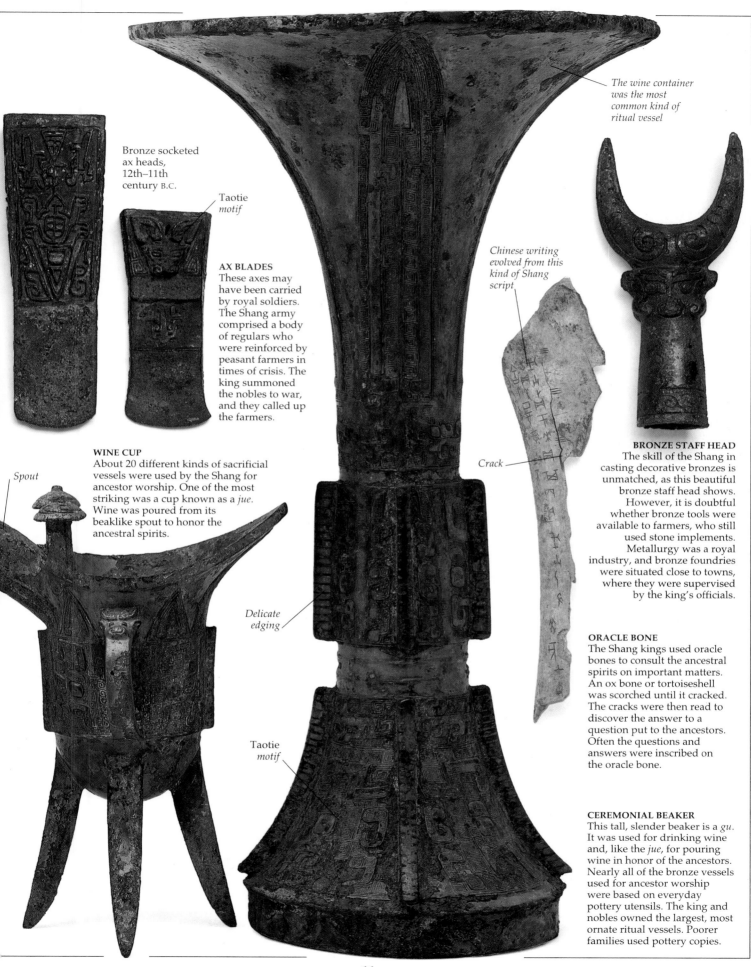

Bronze socketed ax heads, 12th–11th century B.C.

Taotie motif

AX BLADES
These axes may have been carried by royal soldiers. The Shang army comprised a body of regulars who were reinforced by peasant farmers in times of crisis. The king summoned the nobles to war, and they called up the farmers.

Spout

WINE CUP
About 20 different kinds of sacrificial vessels were used by the Shang for ancestor worship. One of the most striking was a cup known as a *jue*. Wine was poured from its beaklike spout to honor the ancestral spirits.

The wine container was the most common kind of ritual vessel

Chinese writing evolved from this kind of Shang script

Crack

Delicate edging

Taotie motif

BRONZE STAFF HEAD
The skill of the Shang in casting decorative bronzes is unmatched, as this beautiful bronze staff head shows. However, it is doubtful whether bronze tools were available to farmers, who still used stone implements. Metallurgy was a royal industry, and bronze foundries were situated close to towns, where they were supervised by the king's officials.

ORACLE BONE
The Shang kings used oracle bones to consult the ancestral spirits on important matters. An ox bone or tortoiseshell was scorched until it cracked. The cracks were then read to discover the answer to a question put to the ancestors. Often the questions and answers were inscribed on the oracle bone.

CEREMONIAL BEAKER
This tall, slender beaker is a *gu*. It was used for drinking wine and, like the *jue*, for pouring wine in honor of the ancestors. Nearly all of the bronze vessels used for ancestor worship were based on everyday pottery utensils. The king and nobles owned the largest, most ornate ritual vessels. Poorer families used pottery copies.

The teachings of Confucius

Large bronze bell, 6th–5th century B.C.

Bell was hung on a loop to allow it to vibrate clearly

CONFUCIUS BELIEVED that the early years of the Zhou dynasty (1027–256 B.C.) were golden years of social harmony. In his own lifetime (551–479 B.C.) Confucius saw only growing disorder. The king's authority was greatly reduced as ambitious lords fought each other for power. This increasing turmoil led Confucius to develop a new moral outlook. It was based on kindness, respect, and the strength of the family. He said that a good ruler should set an example by dealing fairly with his subjects, using force only as a last resort. In return, subjects had a duty to respect and obey their ruler. Confucius believed that family relationships should also be governed by mutual respect, since strong family bonds formed the basis of a stable society. He summed up his philosophy when he said: "Let the prince be a prince, the minister a minister, the father a father, and the son a son." Confucius encouraged ancestor worship because it strengthened family loyalties. As a result, the Chinese came to see themselves as part of a greater family that encompassed not only the living but also the dead and the unborn.

Confucius, the "uncrowned emperor" of China, whose ideas shaped Chinese thought for several milleniums

ZHOU CHIMES
The Chinese believed the music of bells calmed the mind and aided thought. On hearing a piece of ritual music, Confucius was inspired to spurn worldly comforts for three months, living on rice and water.

Bell had no clapper inside; it was struck on the outside like a gong

Ear

Spiky horn

Horselike face

Side view

Zhou bronze ritual vessel, or *gui*, 11th-century B.C.

Handle in the form of a mythical beast

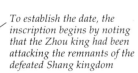

Inscriptions used in ritual vessels evolved into one of the most renowned forms of early Chinese script

Overhead view

RITES OF PASSAGE
Confucius had good reason to regard the first Zhou kings as ideal rulers. After the death of the last Shang king in 1027 B.C., the victorious Zhou leader, Wu, showed proper respect for the fallen royal house by arranging for the continuation of ancestral rites. This sacrificial vessel was used for ancestor worship in the early Zhou period.

To establish the date, the inscription begins by noting that the Zhou king had been attacking the remnants of the defeated Shang kingdom

A MESSAGE TO THE ANCESTORS
An inscription inside this sacrificial vessel records the grant of territory or office to a friend of the Duke of Kang, a brother of the Zhou king Wu. Placing inscriptions inside ritual vessels was common practice among Zhou nobles. They recorded honors and gifts bestowed upon them by the king. The Zhou nobles believed that their ancestors would learn of their achievements when the vessels were used in the rituals of ancestor worship.

A DISTINGUISHED ANCESTOR

Ancestor worship became an important Chinese tradition. Offerings were made to the ancestors at the festival of Qingming once a year. This clay epitaph tablet stood in front of the tomb of Wang Yuanzhi, a senior administrator in the civil service who died in A.D. 571. The tablet served as a reminder to Wang Yuanzhi's descendants of his distinguished career. They would have made offerings before it during Qingming.

Characters incised in clay, then painted red

FEARSOME GUARDIAN

Relatives conducted the annual rite of ancestor worship at the entrance to their ancestor's tomb. From the Han dynasty onward, every wealthy person had a brick-built underground tomb decorated with pressed bricks or wall paintings. The tomb was covered by a mound and enclosed within a sacred area. Ancestor worshipers approached along a spirit path lined with carvings of animals and sometimes humans.

Tomb guardian, or *qitou*, Tang dynasty

Snaky tail

FABULOUS TOMB ANIMAL

Confucius was against slavery and human or animal sacrifices. Under his influence, it became common practice to place pottery figures inside tombs instead of living slaves and animals. This strange pottery animal was found in a tomb that dates from the 4th century A.D. It was probably intended to ward off evil influences.

Painted mane

Cowlike body

Cloven hoof

The art of war

THREE CENTURIES OF BRUTAL WARFARE marked the decline of the Zhou dynasty. The Zhou became unable to control disputes among the feudal lords, and by 481 B.C. China had separated into seven warring states. Battles became large in scale, with crossbowmen, cavalry, armored infantry, and chariots. Thousands of men were killed or wounded. At the battle of Chang Ping in 260 B.C., over a half million men are known to have fallen. During this period Sun Zi wrote *The Art of War*, the world's oldest military handbook, which gave advice to nobles on the practice of warfare. Eventually the northwestern state of Qin was victorious and, in 221 B.C., united the feuding lords under a single empire. The military began to decline in status and the civil service grew in importance. The gentler ideas of Confucianism prevailed.

Guan Di, the Confucian god of war, worshipped for his ability to prevent conflicts as well as for his heroic character

Harness ornament fitted along the horse's cheek

Gold harness ornaments with *taotie* design, 7th–6th century B.C.

HARNESS ORNAMENTS
These ornate harness attachments decorated the the harnesses of cavalry horses. Although battles largely became contests between massed ranks of foot soldiers, or infantry, the cavalry were still used for lightning attacks and for the defense of the infantry's flanks.

Bronze horse bit, Han dynasty

Bronze noseguard for a chariot horse

Taotie, *or monster face, decoration*

Scabbard and dagger, 7th–6th century B.C.

SWORDPLAY
Military success was displayed in fine weapons, such as this bronze dagger and sword. However, bronze weapons never achieved the status the medieval sword did in Europe. In imperial China, peaceful Confucian virtues were revered over the art of warfare.

SHOW OF STRENGTH
This horse frontlet fitted along the nose of a chariot horse. Both harnesses and chariots were decorated to heighten the magnificent spectacle of the chariots in battle. These splendid vehicles were important status symbols. They were buried with their owners, along with the horses and charioteers.

Bronze axle cap protected the axle of a chariot wheel

HORSEPOWER
This delicate bit was probably worn by a cavalry horse in the Han dynasty. Chinese cavalrymen rode the small Mongolian pony until the Han emperor Wu Di obtained bigger horses from Central Asia in 101 B.C. This greatly improved the cavalry. The larger horses were faster and could carry men who were more heavily armored.

ANCIENT AXLE CAPS
Chariots were made of wood and were pulled by two or four horses. Their wheels raised them high above the ground. They usually carried three men: a charioteer, an archer, and a halberdier. The management of a chariot was considered an essential skill for a noble.

Sword, 4th century B.C.

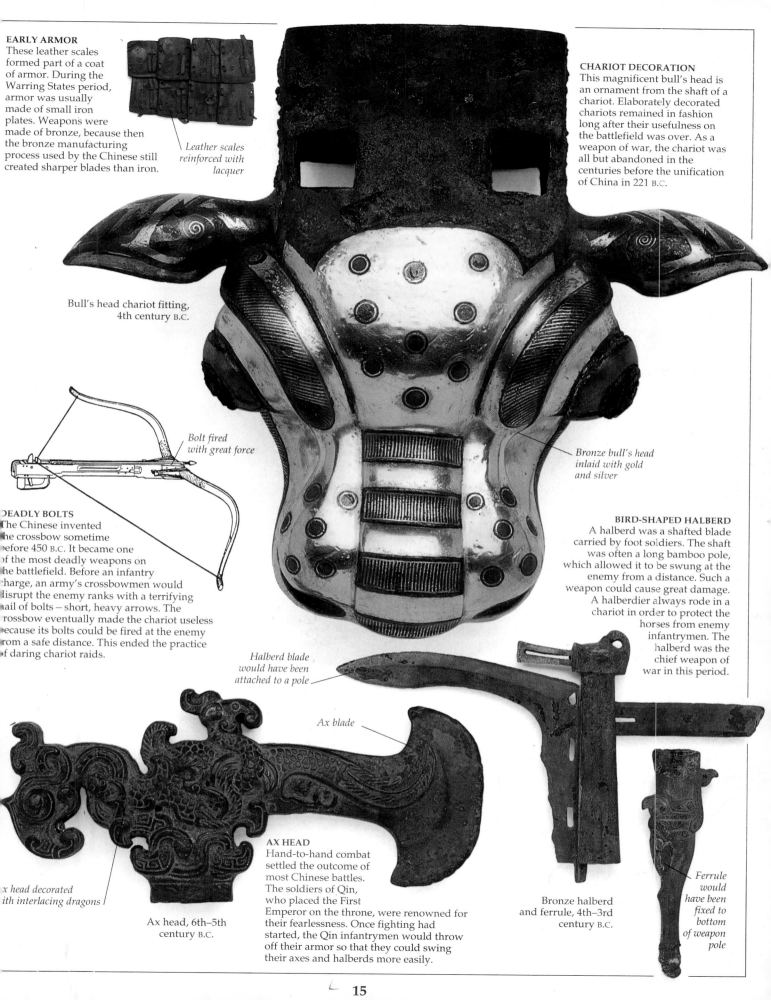

EARLY ARMOR
These leather scales formed part of a coat of armor. During the Warring States period, armor was usually made of small iron plates. Weapons were made of bronze, because then the bronze manufacturing process used by the Chinese still created sharper blades than iron.

Leather scales reinforced with lacquer

Bull's head chariot fitting, 4th century B.C.

DEADLY BOLTS
The Chinese invented the crossbow sometime before 450 B.C. It became one of the most deadly weapons on the battlefield. Before an infantry charge, an army's crossbowmen would disrupt the enemy ranks with a terrifying hail of bolts – short, heavy arrows. The crossbow eventually made the chariot useless because its bolts could be fired at the enemy from a safe distance. This ended the practice of daring chariot raids.

Bolt fired with great force

CHARIOT DECORATION
This magnificent bull's head is an ornament from the shaft of a chariot. Elaborately decorated chariots remained in fashion long after their usefulness on the battlefield was over. As a weapon of war, the chariot was all but abandoned in the centuries before the unification of China in 221 B.C.

Bronze bull's head inlaid with gold and silver

BIRD-SHAPED HALBERD
A halberd was a shafted blade carried by foot soldiers. The shaft was often a long bamboo pole, which allowed it to be swung at the enemy from a distance. Such a weapon could cause great damage. A halberdier always rode in a chariot in order to protect the horses from enemy infantrymen. The halberd was the chief weapon of war in this period.

Halberd blade would have been attached to a pole

Ax blade

Ax head decorated with interlacing dragons

Ax head, 6th–5th century B.C.

AX HEAD
Hand-to-hand combat settled the outcome of most Chinese battles. The soldiers of Qin, who placed the First Emperor on the throne, were renowned for their fearlessness. Once fighting had started, the Qin infantrymen would throw off their armor so that they could swing their axes and halberds more easily.

Bronze halberd and ferrule, 4th–3rd century B.C.

Ferrule would have been fixed to bottom of weapon pole

The first emperor of China

Jade dragon ornaments; the dragon was the adopted symbol of the First Emperor

IN 221 B.C. THE CHINESE EMPIRE was formed. The Qin soldiers defeated the last of their enemies and united the "warring states" under one leader, Zheng. To show his supremacy over the kings he had vanquished, Zheng took the title First Sovereign Qin Emperor, or Qin Shi Huangdi. The empire took its name from the Qin (pronounced "Chin") to become China. The First Emperor (221–207 B.C.) seems to have thought he would become immortal. He built an impressive tomb guarded by thousands of life-size terra-cotta warriors, probably in the belief that he would remain a powerful man in the afterlife. His brief reign on earth was harsh. He used his subjects as slave laborers to build the Great Wall and suppressed anyone who disagreed with him. But after the First Emperor's rule, the Chinese felt that unity was normal.

A CELESTIAL RULER?
The brief reign of the First Emperor left a permanent impression on Chinese society. But he ruled his subjects harshly and his dynasty was overthrown by a peasant rebellion in 207 B.C., just three years after his death.

THE TERRA-COTTA ARMY
The ghostly army of terra-cotta soldiers that guards the First Emperor's tomb is accompanied by life-size horses and chariots. No two soldiers have the same face – each is an individual portrait of a soldier from the Qin army. The soldiers once carried real weapons, but these were stolen by grave robbers after the fall of the Qin.

Embroidered roundel, probably used on a 19th-century imperial robe

Clouds

Waves

WHAT'S IN A NAME?
This is the beginning of an inscription celebrating the unification of China by the First Emperor in 221 B.C. The top character is part of the First Emperor's title. It conveys the idea of divinity, or divine favor.

THE BURNING OF THE BOOKS
When scholars disagreed with his harsh acts, the First Emperor burned their books and executed those who spoke against him. He was particularly displeased with followers of Confucius who pointed out how his policies differed from the ways of old. In 213 B.C., his chief minister announced: "No one is to use the past to discredit the present." Only books on agriculture, medicine, and oracles were spared the flames.

THE DRAGON KING
The association of Chinese emperors with the dragon was undoubtedly due to the First Emperor. The dragon became his emblem because the dragon was the divine lord of the waters, and water was the lucky element for the Qin.

GREAT BUILDING WORKS
The First Emperor used the forced labor of his subjects to carry out his extensive public works. These included the Great Wall, roads, and canals. The hardship suffered by the thousands of men who toiled on the Great Wall is still recalled in Chinese folksongs. To fund his projects, the First Emperor taxed his subjects heavily, which led to widespread suffering and starvation.

THE GREAT WALL OF CHINA
The First Emperor's greatest achievement was the construction of the Great Wall in about 214 B.C. It joined together a number of defensive walls aimed at keeping out the Xiongnu nomads. It is the longest structure ever built.

DRAGON CHARACTERISTICS
A Chinese dragon has the head of a camel, the horns of a stag, the eyes of a demon, the scales of a fish, the claws of an eagle, the pads of a tiger, the ears of a bull, and the long whiskers of a cat. It can make itself as small as a silkworm or large enough to overshadow the world.

Scaly skin

Staglike horns

Fierce eyes

Long whiskers

Clouds

THE IMPERIAL DRAGON
Paradoxically, the First Emperor chose a benevolent being as his favoured deity. The Chinese dragon, or *long*, is not a terrifying monster but a benign creature that embodies wisdom, strength, and goodness. Above all, the dragon symbolizes the life-giving force of water. The ancient Chinese believed that dragons inhabited every river, lake, and sea and also lived high in the sky among the rainclouds.

Pearl of wisdom

The five-clawed dragon was the symbol of the emperor

Imperial seal with a dragon surrounded by clouds guarding the pearl of wisdom, 14th-century

In the empire's service

THE EARLIEST MEMBERS of the imperial civil service were recruited by Gaozu (206–195 B.C.), the first Han emperor. Gaozu led one of the peasant armies that overthrew the Qin dynasty in 207 B.C. Although Gaozu was uneducated, when he came to power he realized the empire needed educated administrators. He gathered together scholars to form an imperial civil service, which was destined to run China for 2,000 years. In 124 B.C. the Han emperor Wu Di (140–87 B.C.) introduced examinations for civil servants and founded an imperial university, where candidates studied the ancient Confucian classics. In later dynasties, a series of examinations took successful candidates from their local districts, through the provinces, to the imperial palace. Those who passed the top palace examinations could expect to be appointed as ministers or even marry princesses.

THE MOMENT OF TRUTH
These local magistrates are taking part in a civil service examination. At each level, only a few candidates passed. They answered questions on the Confucian classics, whose 431, 286 words had to be learned by heart. Reform of the curriculum was strongly opposed and it hardly changed through the centuries.

Long beard associated with old age and wisdom

19TH-CENTURY EXAM PAPER
This test paper shows a candidate's answer and his tutor's comments. Those who studied for an official career knew it involved long years of preparation, but the rewards were great. On receiving his results, an 8th-century graduate called Meng Jiao remarked: "The drudgery of yesterday is forgotten. Today the prospects are vast, and my heart is filled with joy!"

A WISE OFFICIAL
Qiu Jun, above, was a Ming official who persuaded the emperor to strengthen the Great Wall against the Manchus. His advice was well-founded. The Manchus invaded China in 1644.

18th-century figure in official garb

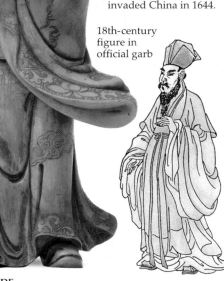

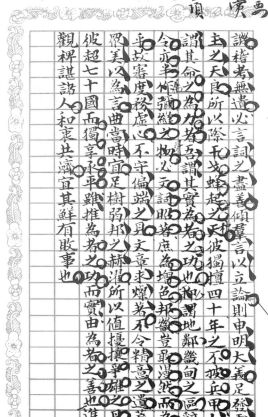

Circles indicate praise for calligraphy

THE PASSING PARADE
The special slate or document held by this official would have been carried on formal occasions, such as the splendid graduation ceremony of successful examination candidates. In the imperial palace, top graduates received their degrees and bowed to the emperor.

A NEW CURRICULUM
The Song minister Wang Anshi, above, altered the civil service examinations so that a mastery of technical subjects would be favored over learning by heart. This reform lasted only briefly.

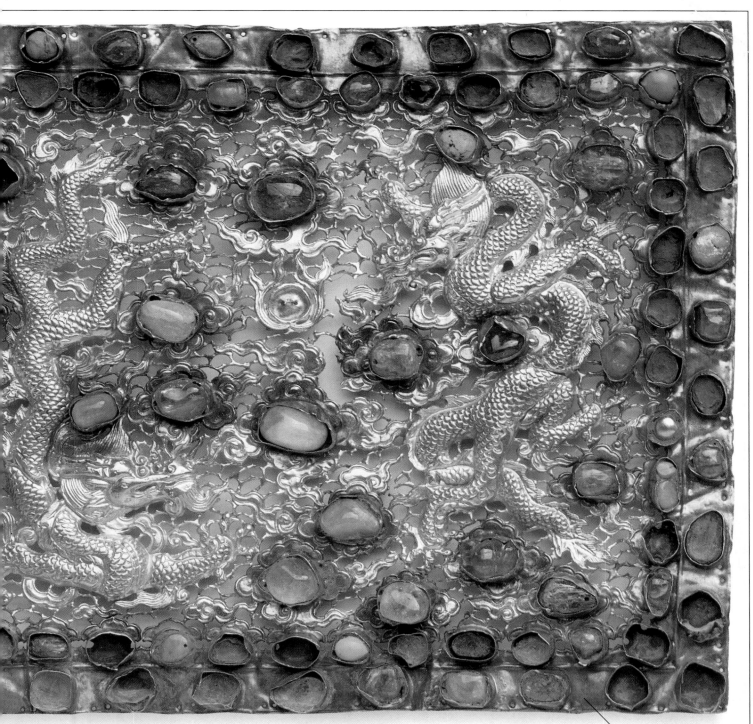

Plaque was sewn onto official robes

OFFICIAL PLAQUE
This beautiful gold plaque is decorated with imperial five-clawed dragons and semiprecious stones. Such an expensive badge of rank may have been worn by an imperial minister or a prince during the Ming dynasty.

THE DANGERS OF CHEATING
A handkerchief covered with model exam answers would have made a clever crib. However, cheating in the imperial examinations was not only difficult but dangerous. Candidates took the provincial examinations in open-doored cells inside walled compounds. Soldiers in watchtowers made sure that no cribs were smuggled in. When the emperor Xian Feng learned of cheating in the palace examinations of 1859, he beheaded the examiners responsible for the cheating, banished the administrators, and took away the qualifications of the guilty graduates.

19

Continued on next page

A civil service career

Graduate civil servants had secured jobs in the most honorable and best rewarded career in China. They took posts in local, provincial, or national government. Competition to join the civil service became so intense during the final centuries of the empire that the odds against succeeding in the palace examinations were as high as 3,000 to one.

A PREFECT IN HIS COURT
The bulk of the work in the civil service was carried out in the local districts, or prefectures, by prefects. A prefect, or *ling,* had to enforce law and order, register individuals and property, collect taxes, store grain against times of famine, organize labor for public works, supervise schools, and judge civil and criminal cases. The area for which a prefect was responsible consisted of a walled city or town and its surrounding villages and farmland.

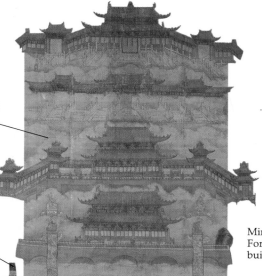

Celestial clouds

Senior official

COURT NECKLACE
The clothes and jewelry worn by officials were an indication of rank and therefore followed strict guidelines. The kind of necklace above was worn only by officials in the top five ranks during the Qing dynasty. The design was based on the Buddhist rosary.

Subsidiary string of 10 beads

Large beads called Buddha heads divide the smaller beads into groups of 27

Ming painting on silk of the Forbidden City, which was built in the early 15th century

Ivory court necklace, early 20th century

An official greets others outside the gates of the Forbidden City

Cap made of black velvet

Bronze finial

GATEWAY FOR THE CHOSEN FEW
This painting shows the Forbidden City, the splendid palace built in Beijing by the Ming emperor Yong Lo. Only senior officials and ministers could enter its Meridian Gate, seen here with its triple archways. The most senior official in the empire was called the Grand Tutor in deference to Confucius.

BADGE OF RANK
The rank of this military official from the Qing dynasty is indicated by the embroidered badge on the front of his surcoat, or *pufu.* His tiger insignia shows that he was a fourth-rank official.

OFFICIAL HEADWARE
Once the Qing dynasty was firmly established, the black hat with side flaps worn by Ming civil servants was replaced by the Manchu cap. This cap had a finial to indicate rank; it could be made of bronze, glass, crystal, coral, or jade.

MASSED RANKS
The size of the civil service under the different dynasties is not always clear. However, it is known for certain that in the Han dynasty the civil service contained 135,285 officials, including all ranks, high and low. By the Ming dynasty this number had grown to 180,000. When officials were crowded together, it was often difficult to see which ranks they belonged to. Therefore, from the Ming dynasty onward, the rank of a civil servant was indicated by a large badge sewn onto his surcoat. Each of the nine ranks of the civil service was identified by a different bird. These two badges are from the Qing dynasty. The white crane, above, was the official insignia of the first rank, and the egret, right, signified the sixth.

SEAL OF APPROVAL
Every document in China was stamped with a seal. This 18th-century bronze seal belonged to the civil service department responsible for supplying water to the capital, Beijing. It is inscribed with both Manchu and Chinese scripts, a reminder of the foreign origin of the last imperial house, the Manchu, or Qing, dynasty.

A land of invention

Pocket compass

SOME OF THE WORLD'S GREATEST INVENTIONS came from China. Throughout its imperial history, emperors encouraged the development of science and technology, and for centuries China led other nations in these areas. In the Middle Ages many Chinese inventions were carried along the Silk Road to Europe, where some had an enormous impact. In time, paper and printing dramatically improved communications; gunpowder changed the way in which battles were fought; a harness for draft animals revolutionized agriculture; and boats equipped with the magnetic compass, the sternpost rudder, and watertight buoyancy chambers were able to embark on great voyages of discovery. Other Chinese inventions that made the world a different place were paper money, clockwork, silk, porcelain, fireworks, kites, umbrellas, and the wheelbarrow.

A WATER-POWERED BLAST FURNACE
China was the first country in the world to develop iron casting, in the 6th century B.C. This skill was refined in the 1st century A.D. by an unknown official who invented a water powered metallurgical blowing machine. The machine, pictured on the left, produced a steady blast of heat that greatly improved cast iron production. It helped increase the output of the state-owned iron industry and may have led to the first production of steel.

THE "EARTHQUAKE WEATHERCOCK"
The first instrument for monitoring earthquakes was invented in A.D. 130 by Zhang Heng, director of astrology in the late Han court. Zhang Heng's invention, below, could detect an earthquake and indicate its direction from the capital, Luoyang. The original apparatus was a huge bronze machine that measured 6 feet (2 meters) across. An earthquake tremor caused a mechanism inside the machine to release a ball from the side of the machine farthest away from the earthquake's epicenter. This notified the emperor of the direction of the disaster.

FINDING THE RIGHT DIRECTION
The magnetic compass was an ancient Chinese invention. Compasses were first used in town planning to make sure that new houses faced in a direction that was deemed to be in harmony with nature. Later the compass was used for navigation at sea. These 19th-century compasses are from the port of Canton.

The longer the handles of a wheelbarrow, the less force needed to lift the load

Bronze ball released from dragon's mouth

Toad catches the ball

ASTRONOMICAL CLOCKWORK
Between 1088 and 1092, a civil servant named Su Song built the first mechanical clock. It told the time of day and tracked the heavenly bodies so that accurate horoscopes could be drawn. The clockwork was driven by the flow of water into the buckets on a waterwheel. As each bucket filled it tilted a lever, the next bucket advanced, and the wheel turned at a precise rate. The clockwork was housed in a large tower. In front, revolving figures appeared at windows to chime the hours. An inside platform housed a celestial globe, and an armillary sphere for monitoring celestial objects sat on the roof.

Armillary sphere

Puppet holds up a plaque telling the time

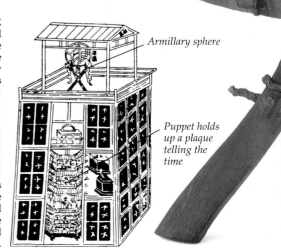

STEERING A STRAIGHT COURSE

The sternpost rudder was invented between 205 B.C. and A.D. 220. It made the steering of large vessels possible for the first time. Chinese junks of 1,500 tons could carry huge loads long before such large ships were built in Europe.

Shield to protect soldier

Multiple gun releases a hail of bullets

GUNPOWDER

Chinese alchemists discovered gunpowder in the 8th century while they were carrying out experiments to find the elixir of life. By the 10th century, gunpowder was being used to make fireworks and weapons. The Chinese invented the gun, the rocket, the bomb, and the mine. The Song army used guns against the invading Mongols in the early 13th century, but they were eventually overpowered by the greater might of the Mongol empire.

Ming soldier firing a multiple gun

Ocean-going junk

Rudder

One-dollar note, 1906

Basket for carrying loads

THE PAPER REVOLUTION

Papermaking was perfected in China in A.D. 105 by an imperial official called Cai Lun. The first paper was made from pulped silk waste. Later hemp, bark, or bamboo were used. Paper was a necessary forerunner of widescale printing, and it played an important part in the spread of books and the growth of literacy in China. Paper money first appeared in the 11th century.

The wheelbarrow was sometimes fitted with a sail to harness wind power

THE WHEELBARROW

The Chinese invented the wheelbarrow between 221 B.C. and A.D. 265 during the period of the Three Kingdoms. This large handcart enabled a single person to transport a heavy load, which led to its Chinese name, the "wooden ox."

A sturdy wheel lifts the load above the ground

Paper, printing, and books

PAPER AND PRINTING were possibly the most important Chinese inventions. Credit for the successful manufacture of paper is given to Cai Lun, head of the imperial workshops in A.D. 105. The first paper was made from silk rags; later other fibrous materials were used, such as bamboo, hemp, and mulberry bark. There was a great demand for paper from the Han civil service, and it was mass-produced in government factories. Large-scale woodblock printing was developed in the 9th century, increasing the availability of reading material. By the end of the Tang dynasty, bookshops were trading in every Chinese city. Movable type was invented by a printer called Bi Sheng in the Song dynasty, but because at least 80,000 separate type symbols were needed, it did not entirely replace block printing.

Bamboo symbolized strength and flexibility

BAMBOO BOOKS
The first Chinese books were made from strips of bamboo, such as those at right, which were tied together in a bundle. These early books were unwieldy to use and took up a lot of storage space.

PAPERMAKING
Before the papermaking process could begin, the raw material was softened by being soaked in water. After that, it was boiled and pounded to form a pulp. To make a sheet of paper, a fine screen was dipped into the pulp to gather a thin film of fibers. The screen was pressed to remove the water, then left to dry on a heated wall. When dry, the finished sheet of paper was peeled off the screen.

Soaking the bamboo

Dipping the screen in the vat

Pressing the screen to remove the water

SEAL PRINTS
Seals, which date back to the Zhou dynasty, were the first form of printing used in China. They were impressed on official documents, personal correspondence, and works of art. Seals were carved or molded from stone, wood, horn, bronze, or ceramics. This 15th-century soapstone seal was engraved by a famous Ming calligrapher.

PAPER MOLD
Chinese papermakers used paper molds like this one, which consists of a fine bamboo screen set in a wooden frame. The mold was dipped into a vat of mushy pulp and shaken gently to settle the fibers onto the screen. The screen was then taken out and pressed to remove the excess water before being left to dry.

WOODBLOCK PRINTING
From the 9th century onward, the Chinese printed books from large wooden blocks. The text of either one or two pages was carved into a block by first pasting a thin manuscript over it and then cutting through the paper. The characters were carved in reverse. A print was taken by inking the surface of the block, laying a piece of paper over it, and rubbing gently with a dry brush.

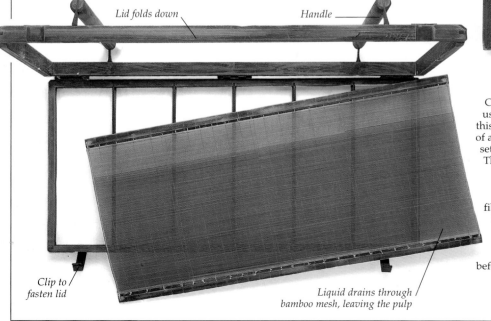

Lid folds down

Handle

Clip to fasten lid

Liquid drains through bamboo mesh, leaving the pulp

Text reads top down, from right to left

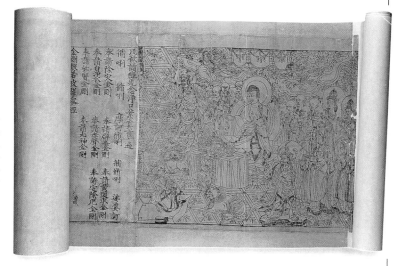

ON A SCROLL
The first Chinese books made of paper were rolled into long scrolls. They were usually handwritten by scholars. As in modern China, the text was written in vertical columns and read from right to left.

PRAYERS IN PRINT
This Buddhist text, called the *Diamond Sutra*, is the earliest known printed book. It was made in China in A.D. 868 using woodblock printing. Buddhists produced thousands of copies of sacred texts and prayers. The *Diamond Sutra* was made for free distribution.

Book cover decorated with colorful chrysanthemums

STYLISH NOTEPAPER
This collection of decorated letter papers is a fine example of colored woodblock printing, which flourished in 16th-century China. It was produced by the Ten Bamboo Studio in 1644. Scholars used beautifully designed letter papers for decorative letters. The delicate illustrations were intended to be written over.

20th-century facsimile of a compendium of letter papers from the Ten Bamboo Studio

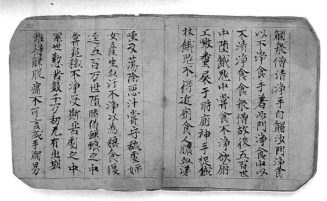

EMERGENCY MANUAL
Large-scale printing in the 10th century made books readily available in China for the first time. The spread of books greatly increased the spread of literacy. The most popular printed material was Buddhist texts and prayers. This 1,000-year-old booklet contains a Buddhist prayer called the *Lotus Sutra*. It is a prayer for use in emergencies that calls on the help of friendly spirits.

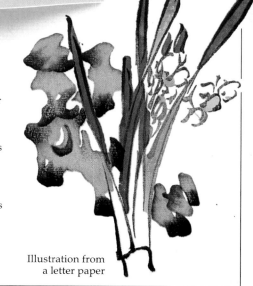

Illustration from a letter paper

The Three Ways

IN IMPERIAL CHINA, RELIGIOUS BELIEFS were divided into the "three ways" of Confucianism, Daoism, and Buddhism. Throughout its long history, China was tolerant of all religions. Although there were disagreements over religious principles, few people were persecuted for their beliefs. In this respect, the Chinese empire was unique among civilizations. Confucianism and Daoism emerged in the Warring States period. Against the backdrop of constant warfare, these two religions encouraged more peaceful ways of being. Buddhism came to China from India in the 1st century A.D., and its gentle teachings became popular in the troubled centuries that followed the end of the Han dynasty. The return of strong government under the Tang emperors (618–906) led to the decline of Buddhism and the revival of Confucianism. Nevertheless, Buddhism had taken firm root in Chinese culture and became China's most popular belief.

Legend has it that Lao Zi was born aged 70

LAO ZI
Daoists were followers of Lao Zi , or "the Old Philosopher" (born c. 604 B.C.), who believed that people should live in harmony with nature. He explained his ideas in a book called the *Daodejing*. Lao Zi wanted people to lead simple lives that did not disrupt the balance of the natural world. He disliked the importance Confucius placed on duty to family and state because he did not believe in regulations. Daoism was represented by the yin yang sign, which reflects natural harmony.

Zhongli Quan, chief of the eight immortals; he could raise the dead with a wave of his fan

Fan with a tortoise, a symbol of luck and wisdom

Flute

Sacred scroll

THE GENTLE PROTECTOR
Kuanyin was the Buddhist goddess of mercy. Her name means "she who hears prayers," and she is often portrayed as the protector of children. Kuanyin was a Chinese transformation of the Indian male god Avalokitesvara. This is just one of the many changes the Chinese made to Indian Buddhism. In China, Kuanyin was the greatest Buddhist deity.

THE HEIGHT OF BEAUTY
A pagoda is a sacred Buddhist tower. Pagodas have from three to 15 tiers and are usually exquisitely decorated. The Chinese believed that a pagoda brought good fortune to the area surrounding it.

Zhang Guolao an immortal who could make himself invisible

Han Xiangzi, patron of musicians, who could make flowers blossom instantly

THE MYSTERIES OF THE IMMORTALS
Daoists thought that it was possible to discover the elixir of life and become immortal. They worshiped eight figures whom they believed had achieved immortality. These mysterious immortals, or *xian*, lived in remote mountains. They were said to have supernatural powers, such as the power to turn objects into gold, become invisible, make flowers bloom instantly, or raise the dead.

Ivory figures, Ming dynasty, 16th–17th century

A GUIDE TO ETERNAL PEACE
A Bodhisattva, or "enlightened being," is a godlike personage. Bodhisattvas had postponed their own hope of eternal peace, or nirvana, to help other people. Kuanyin, the goddess of mercy, was the greatest Chinese Bodhisattva, but there were many others that Buddhists could call upon when they needed help.

Crowned stucco head of a Bodhisattva, 8th–9th century A.D.

Head blends male and female features; note the dainty half-mustache

CONFUCIUS
The great Chinese thinker Confucius (551–479 B.C.) taught people to show respect for one another. He said that a good ruler should cherish his subjects and they should honour him. He also believed that respect within the family was very important because a stable society was based on strong families. The Daoists did not agree with Confucius. In his own defence Confucius said, "They dislike me because I want to reform society, but if we are not to live with our fellow men with whom can we live? We cannot live with animals. If society was as it ought to be, I should not seek to change it."

Modern Buddhist image for domestic use

Halo shows the emanation of holiness from the Buddha

Buddha seated on a sacred lotus

BUDDHA
Buddhists follow the teachings of Buddha (born c. 563 B.C.), a north Indian prince who devoted his life to a search for personal peace, or enlightenment. The name means "enlightened one." He believed that by giving up worldly desires, such as for fine food and clothes, a blissful state called nirvana could be achieved. In nirvana there was freedom from the sorrows of the world. Indian belief at that time held that people were reborn many times. Persons who had lived badly in former lives might be reborn in animal or insect form. Buddha said that by reaching nirvana, this endless cycle of rebirth could be broken.

Health and medicine

TRADITIONAL CHINESE MEDICINE is based on the use of herbs, acupuncture, and a balanced diet. It combines ancient philosophy with practical skills. According to Chinese belief, a person falls ill when the two opposing forces of yin and yang become unbalanced in the body. Doctors use acupuncture and herbal remedies to rechannel these natural energies. Chinese interest in medicine dates back more than 4,000 years. In ancient times, the Daoists believed that it was possible to find the elixir of life, which would make people immortal. Concern with health also came from the need to produce strong sons who would ensure the survival of the family. From the Tang dynasty onward, Chinese doctors were regularly examined on their medical expertise. In 1111, the entire knowledge of the medical profession was compiled in a vast encyclopedia. This great work listed all the known diseases, with their symptoms, diagnoses, and treatments. It became the standard reference book for Chinese medicine.

Licorice root, or *gan cao*

Chinese hawthorn, or *shan zha*

Smoked plums, or *wu mei*

VITAL NOURISHMENT
The Chinese have always believed a balanced diet to be the basis of good health. The ingredients above make up a nourishing herbal drink said to improve the appetite and clear the chest.

Coin sword from the Qing dynasty, placed by the bed of a sick person to ward off bad spirits

10th-century acupuncture chart showing some of the main needle points in the arm

TAPPING THE LIFE FORCE
Acupuncture has been used to treat illnesses for more than 2,000 years. It is based on the belief that the life force of the body flows along 12 meridians, or lines. Each meridian is linked to a different organ in the body. An acupuncturist inserts needles at various points along these meridians to relieve pain or treat illness.

Cap screws securely into case

Set of eight steel acupuncture needles, Qing dynasty

HEAT TREATMENT
Moxibustion is a pain-relief treatment that uses heat produced by burning dried mugwort, or *moxa*. Acupuncture and moxibustion are often used together. An acupuncture needle can be fitted with a small cap in which *moxa* is burned. The heat is carried into the body by the needle. Burning *moxa* sticks can also be used to apply heat to points along the meridian.

Moxa stick

Moxa wool

Moxa *burned in cap*

NATURAL PAIN RELIEF
This set of needles belonged to a 19th-century acupuncturist. In the 20th century, doctors have discovered that acupuncture can be used as an anesthetic for surgery. When acupuncture is used during an operation, the patient remains conscious and feels little or no pain. Scientists believe acupuncture works by stimulating the release of endorphins, the brain's natural painkillers.

Mahogany case for storing needles

Modern acupuncture needles with a cap for *moxa* wool

Lighted end of moxa stick is held over painful area

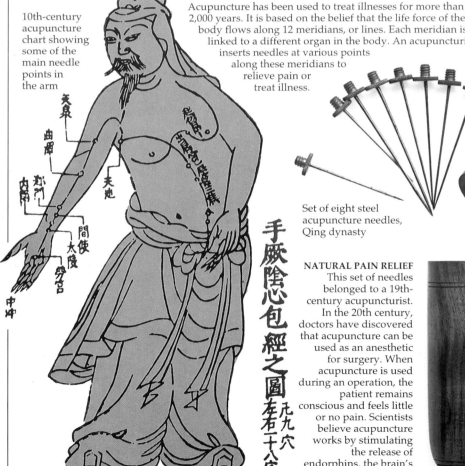

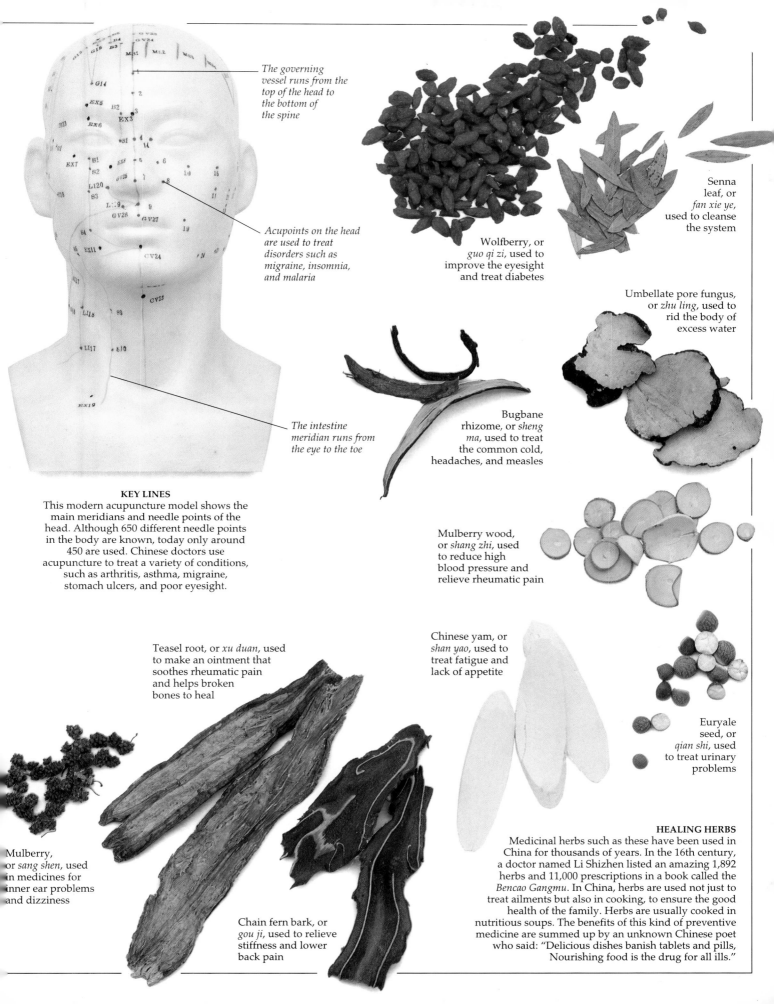

The governing vessel runs from the top of the head to the bottom of the spine

Acupoints on the head are used to treat disorders such as migraine, insomnia, and malaria

Wolfberry, or *guo qi zi*, used to improve the eyesight and treat diabetes

Senna leaf, or *fan xie ye*, used to cleanse the system

Umbellate pore fungus, or *zhu ling*, used to rid the body of excess water

Bugbane rhizome, or *sheng ma*, used to treat the common cold, headaches, and measles

The intestine meridian runs from the eye to the toe

KEY LINES
This modern acupuncture model shows the main meridians and needle points of the head. Although 650 different needle points in the body are known, today only around 450 are used. Chinese doctors use acupuncture to treat a variety of conditions, such as arthritis, asthma, migraine, stomach ulcers, and poor eyesight.

Mulberry wood, or *shang zhi*, used to reduce high blood pressure and relieve rheumatic pain

Chinese yam, or *shan yao*, used to treat fatigue and lack of appetite

Teasel root, or *xu duan*, used to make an ointment that soothes rheumatic pain and helps broken bones to heal

Euryale seed, or *qian shi*, used to treat urinary problems

Mulberry, or *sang shen*, used in medicines for inner ear problems and dizziness

Chain fern bark, or *gou ji*, used to relieve stiffness and lower back pain

HEALING HERBS
Medicinal herbs such as these have been used in China for thousands of years. In the 16th century, a doctor named Li Shizhen listed an amazing 1,892 herbs and 11,000 prescriptions in a book called the *Bencao Gangmu*. In China, herbs are used not just to treat ailments but also in cooking, to ensure the good health of the family. Herbs are usually cooked in nutritious soups. The benefits of this kind of preventive medicine are summed up by an unknown Chinese poet who said: "Delicious dishes banish tablets and pills, Nourishing food is the drug for all ills."

The three perfections

CALLIGRAPHY, POETRY, AND PAINTING were known as the "three perfections." The combination of these arts was considered the height of artistic expression. They were usually combined in the form of a poetically inspired landscape painting with beautiful calligraphy running down one side. From the Song dynasty (960–1279) onward, the practice of the three perfections was seen as the greatest accomplishment of an educated person. The Song emperor Hui Zong (1101–25) led the way toward transforming writing into an art form. He developed an elegant style of calligraphy called "slender gold." Hui Zong was also a gifted poet and painter, and the arts flourished under his reign.

IN THE BEGINNING
Legend has it that Chinese writing was invented over 4,000 years ago by Cang Jie, an official of the mythical Yellow Emperor. He devised written characters from the tracks of birds and animals. The legend says that "all the spirits cried out in agony, as the innermost secrets of nature were revealed."

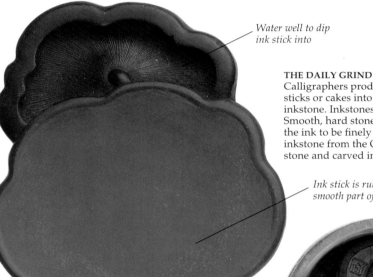

Water well to dip ink stick into

THE DAILY GRIND
Calligraphers produced their own ink by grinding ink sticks or cakes into a small amount of water on an inkstone. Inkstones were made from stone or pottery. Smooth, hard stones were favored because they allowed the ink to be finely ground to make smooth ink. This inkstone from the Qing dynasty is made from Duan stone and carved in the shape of two fungi.

Soft, springy brush tip probably made of wolf hair

Ink stick is rubbed on the smooth part of the inkstone

Ink cake decorated with a legendary animal

Classical garden depicted in mother-of-pearl inlay

Box lined with tortoiseshell

CARBON COPY
Ink was made by mixing pine soot with lampblack obtained from other burned plants. This mixture was combined with animal glue and molded into a stick or cake. Ink sticks and cakes were often decorated with calligraphy or molded into the shapes of dragons and birds copied from mythology.

19th-century ink box

COLORED INKS
Both calligraphers and painters used inks. In the Song dynasty, colored inks were made by adding such materials as pearl powder, ground jade, and camphor to the ink. Later other pigments were used: indigo for blue, lead for white, cinnabar for red, and malachite for green.

A TREASURED POSSESSION
This beautiful writing brush from the Ming dynasty is made of lacquered wood and inlaid with mother-of-pearl. It was usual for everyday writing implements to be highly decorated. In the 10th century the brushes, paper, ink, and inkstone used by a calligrapher became known as "the four treasures of the scholar's studio."

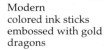

Modern colored ink sticks embossed with gold dragons

This character means "brilliant"; it comes from a poem composed around 1120

All strokes must be drawn gracefully and in the right order

Calligrapher awaits inspiration

DROP BY DROP

This Ming bronze water dropper is in the shape of a boy riding a buffalo. A water dropper was used for wetting the inkstone. It is important to control the supply of water mixed with an ink stick because this affects the tone of the ink. A Tang landscape painter noted that "five colors can be obtained from black ink alone." Calligraphers and painters often had assistants to help prepare ink while they were working.

Porcelain seal-paste box, 19th century

Seal

Impression

BOLD AND BRILLIANT

This is an example of the elegant "slender gold" calligraphy of the Song emperor Hui Zong. For a calligrapher, style was as important as accuracy.

PRACTICE MAKES PERFECT

To become a good calligrapher requires years of practice. Because Chinese writing is based on signs rather than sounds, every sign, or character, must be learned by heart. The strokes that make up each character must be written in the correct sequence. With more than 40,000 characters in the Chinese language, the calligrapher's art is not an easy one.

A GOOD IMPRESSION

Many scholars used a seal as a way of identifying their work. A seal would identify its owner either directly by name or with a favorite quotation. Seal impressions were always printed in red ink. Special paintings might end up covered with different impressions as later admirers and owners affixed their seals to the work.

NATURAL BEAUTY

This stoneware brush washer from the 18th century is cast in the form of a lotus pod. Scholars were uplifted by the beauty of natural forms.

Brush rest in the shape of a three-peaked mountain

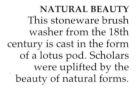

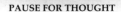

CELESTIAL INSPIRATION

The production of ornamental ink cakes became a minor art form. This octagonal ink cake is decorated with a celestial horse carrying sacred Daoist writings. It was made in 1621 by a famous Ming ink-cake manufacturer called Cheng Dayue. By the time of the Ming dynasty, all educated Chinese people felt they should be skilled in the art of either calligraphy or painting.

PAUSE FOR THOUGHT

A brush rest is an essential item for a calligrapher or painter. This dainty enamel brush rest would have been placed on a writing table. A calligrapher may have used it to hold his writing brush while he awaited inspiration.

Continued on next page

The poetry of landscapes

The soft inks and delicate brushstrokes used in calligraphy were also applied to painting. In the Song dynasty, this technique was used to great effect in the painting of landscapes. Inks created moody, evocative images. For "wet" works that depicted rolling mists or stormy clouds, artists brushed ink washes onto special absorbent paper. The Song emperor Hui Zong added painting to the subjects set in the top civil service examinations. The examination question quoted a line of poetry that had to be illustrated in an original way. Scholars often joined together to demonstrate the three artistic "perfections." One might paint a scene, and another would add a line of poetry in stylish calligraphy.

OFFICIAL POETS
The Song official Su Shi, right, was a famous poet. Many officials were accomplished writers of poetry and prose. Those that studied together were often posted to opposite ends of the empire, but they continued to exchange calligraphy and verse. Their correspondence counts for a great mass of Chinese literature.

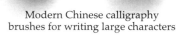

The brush tip contains several different layers of hairs

The inner core of hairs is often waxed to make the brush tip springy

AN EMPEROR'S POEM
This delicate jade bowl stand is carved in the shape of a *bi*, a disk used in ancient rituals. It is inscribed with a poem by the Manchu, or Qing, emperor Qianlong. In the inscription, the emperor says that his "poetic imagination" was stirred by the "subtle and exquisite" shape of the bowl stand and the quality of the jade of which it is made. The foreign emperor Qianlong was a great admirer of Chinese art and collected poems, paintings, and calligraphy from the length and breadth of his empire.

High-quality jade

Goat hair tip

Buffalo horn handle

Carved dragon curls around the pot

Pine tree

Modern Chinese calligraphy brushes for writing large characters

A JADE BRUSH WASHER
The feeling of harmony inspired by classical forms and designs was important to Chinese scholars. Even the humblest objects in a scholar's studio were lovely to look at. This exquisite jade pot was actually used for washing brushes! It is carved with dragons, a favorite Chinese motif, and dates from the Ming dynasty.

Scholar deep in thought

A TRANQUIL SETTING
The scene carved on this 17th-century bamboo brush pot represents a Chinese ideal – a scholar seated quietly underneath a pine tree admiring the beauty of nature.

NATURAL HARMONY

The Song painter Guo Xi believed the main duty of the landscape painter was to bring the peace of nature into every home. A Song landscape painting usually portrayed a tranquil view of mountains and water. Guo Xi said: "When you are planning to paint, you must always create a harmonious relationship between Heaven and Earth."

"Fishing in a mountain stream," by Xu Daoning, ink on silk, 11th century

Wolf hair tip

Bamboo handle

The blue pigment was applied before the glaze

This delicate pattern was painted with a fine brush

THE PERFECT PATTERN

Like all the equipment used by a calligrapher or a painter, this pretty ceramic brush rest is elaborately decorated. The blue pattern is an example of the famous blue-and-white pottery that was first perfected in the Ming dynasty. This brush rest is probably from the late Ming period.

CAPTURED IN BRONZE

This ornate bronze brush rest resembles a classical landscape. It is cast in the shape of a five-peaked mountain range and decorated with plants and animals. The wider central spaces are for holding large brushes.

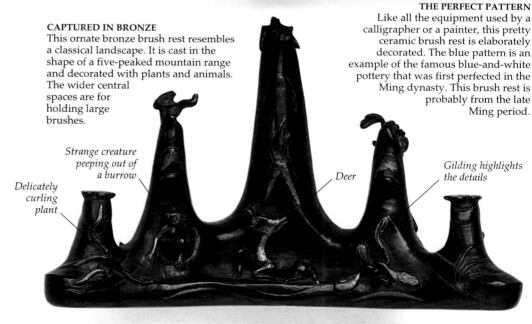

Strange creature peeping out of a burrow

Delicately curling plant

Deer

Gilding highlights the details

DIFFERENT STROKES

A painter or a calligrapher would have a large collection of brushes. Any number of brushes might be required for a landscape painting – large ones for applying a background wash and small ones for picking out detail. A professional calligrapher might need a brush with hair more than a foot long for writing big characters on banners and posters. Brushes were carefully made for these purposes. The hairs of a brush tip could be constructed to produce a soft wash, a firm and even stroke, or a lively, flamboyant line.

Life in the fields

M OST PEOPLE IN IMPERIAL CHINA lived in the countryside and worked in the fields. The hard work of the rural population formed the foundation of the great Chinese empire. The majority of peasant farmers lived on carefully tended family-owned plots of land. Although they were not tied to any lord, they had to pay taxes, serve in the army, and work for a certain number of days each year on public works such as roads and canals. After the great peasant rebellion that toppled the Qin dynasty in 207 B.C., most emperors were careful not to overburden their rural subjects. All the same, the life of a peasant farmer was a hard one. Most farm jobs were carried out by hand, from hoeing the ground to spreading manure. One of the main tasks of a farmer and his family was to maintain and regulate the supply of water to the crops. They transported water by bucket or used irrigation machines that were manually operated. In the hills of northern China, crops were planted on narrow terraces carved into the hillsides. Water was raised to the terraces from wells and canals by human-powered irrigation machines. In the rice-growing regions of southern China, the well-organized irrigation systems created a patchwork landscape of flooded paddy fields.

Chinese painting of the endless chain

Workers chatted to while away the long hours

They balanced on a wooden bar

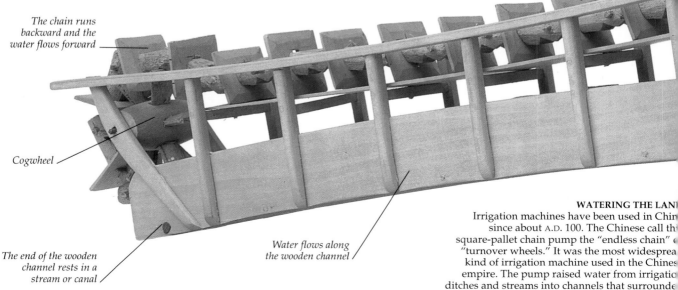

The endless chain of wooden pallets pulls a stream of water uphill

The chain runs backward and the water flows forward

Cogwheel

The end of the wooden channel rests in a stream or canal

Water flows along the wooden channel

WATERING THE LAND
Irrigation machines have been used in China since about A.D. 100. The Chinese call the square-pallet chain pump the "endless chain" or "turnover wheels." It was the most widespread kind of irrigation machine used in the Chinese empire. The pump raised water from irrigation ditches and streams into channels that surrounded the fields. Two people working this machine could irrigate hundreds of plots of land.

Hair worn in a
traditional topknot

The heads of the
workers were often
protected from the
sun by a small roof
(shown in the
painting opposite)

FOOD FOR AN EMPIRE
The mountainous terrain of
northern China is covered with a
rich, yellow soil called loess, which
was originally blown in from the
Mongolian desert. Chinese farmers
cut terraces into the hillsides to
make the most of this fertile land.
They grow millet and wheat in
the long, narrow fields that
wind around the hillsides. In
southern China, farmers grow rice
in the well-irrigated valleys of the
Yangzi River. From the Tang
dynasty onward, the bulk of the
empire's food was grown here.

Threshing

Winnowing

Transporting the grain

The pedals turn a
large cogwheel,
which pulls the
chain of square
wooden pallets

Cogwheel
turns
backward

THE COST OF FAILURE
Every member of a
peasant family had to
work hard on the
farm, particularly at
harvest time. Many
peasant farmers had
to give a large share
of their harvest to a
wealthy landlord, as
well as pay tax to
the emperor. If the
crops failed, a
peasant family
was in danger of
falling into debt
and losing
its land.

The water runs into
an irrigation ditch on
a higher level

35

Continued on next page

Seeds and plowshares

Traditionally peasant farmers used ancient methods of farming, which involved hoeing their crops by hand, transporting water by bucket, and grinding grain with manually operated mills. In the Han dynasty, wealthy farmers built bigger, labor-saving machines powered by water or animals. Iron plowshares pulled by oxen, new irrigation machines, and watermills greatly improved farming output. However, small farmers still relied on human labor. By the Song dynasty, new crop strains and knowledge of fertilizers allowed the peasant farmers in southern China to grow two crops a year in the same field.

REMOVING THE HUSKS
This hand-powered winnowing machine was used to separate the outer shells, or husks, from the grain. Winnowing was traditionally carried out by shaking the grain in a large sieve, then tossing it in the air to remove the husks.

THE HUMAN HAMMER
Harvested grain was crushed by a tilt hammer. This machine was powered by a single man who used his weight to tilt the hammer backward and forward in a seesaw action. There were larger, water-driven tilt hammers in mills near towns and cities.

PLANTING A PADDY FIELD
These peasant farmers are transplanting young rice plants in the soft mud of a paddy field. Originally rice was grown only in flooded paddies. Later, in areas supplied with a good rainfall, farmers cultivated rice in dry fields.

ALL HANDS TO THE HARVEST
This painting from the Yuan dynasty shows a group of peasant farmers harvesting rice. In rural communities, everyone helped with the farm work and women labored alongside men in the fields. Peasant women never had their feet bound because they would have been unable to carry out any kind of field work.

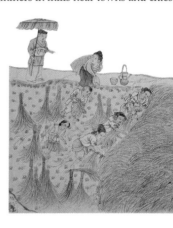

PLOWING THE LAND
During the Han dynasty, government iron foundries began producing plowshares. They were made in various sizes, from large plowshares that were pulled by an oxen team to small, pointed ones that could be used by a single person. According to an ancient Chinese proverb, farmers should always plow their land after rain to conserve the moisture in the ground. The new iron equipment made this backbreaking task much easier.

Hoe

Plow

Tunic probably made of hemp

A LITTLE HELP FROM SOME FRIENDS
This 19th-century model depicts a group of peasant farmers going off to plow their fields. Although every rural family had to support itself, cooperation with friends and neighbors was essential. The upkeep of irrigation ditches and the repair of terraces were tasks shared by the whole village. Larger enterprises were organized by local government. In 111 B.C., the Han emperor Wu Di said: "Agriculture is the basic occupation of the world. So the imperial government must cut canals and ditches, guide the rivers, and build reservoirs in order to prevent flood and drought."

Pot of water or tea for the workers to drink

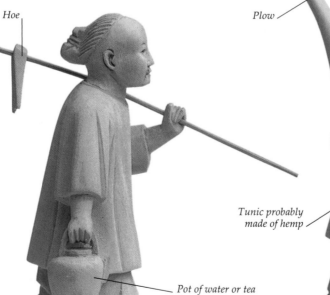

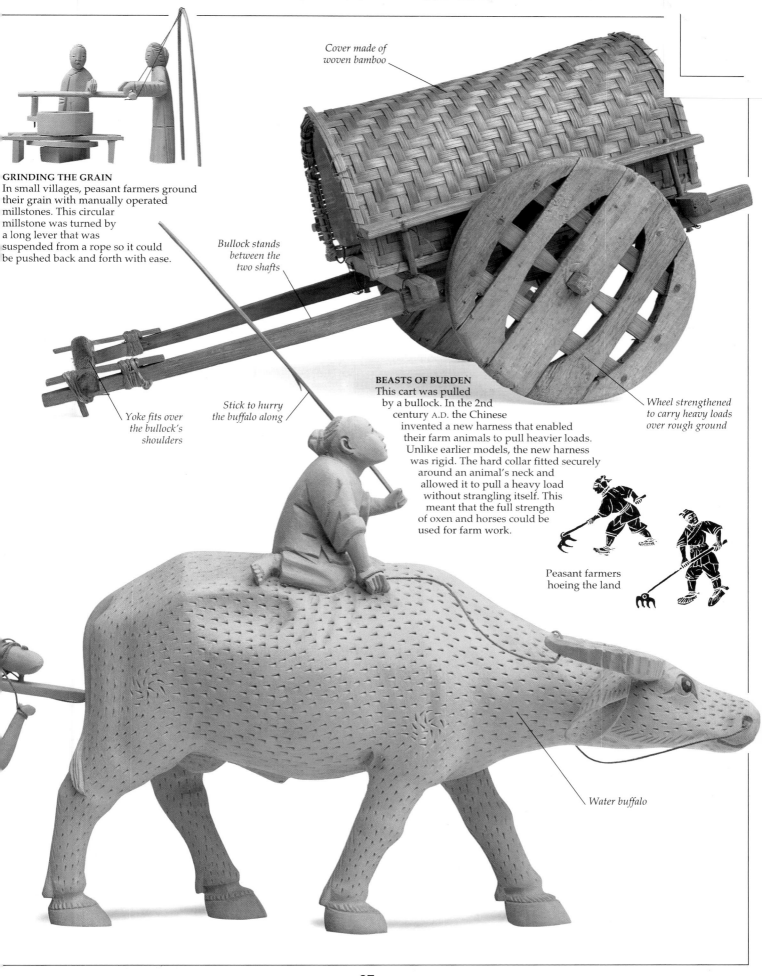

GRINDING THE GRAIN
In small villages, peasant farmers ground their grain with manually operated millstones. This circular millstone was turned by a long lever that was suspended from a rope so it could be pushed back and forth with ease.

Cover made of woven bamboo

Bullock stands between the two shafts

Yoke fits over the bullock's shoulders

Stick to hurry the buffalo along

BEASTS OF BURDEN
This cart was pulled by a bullock. In the 2nd century A.D. the Chinese invented a new harness that enabled their farm animals to pull heavier loads. Unlike earlier models, the new harness was rigid. The hard collar fitted securely around an animal's neck and allowed it to pull a heavy load without strangling itself. This meant that the full strength of oxen and horses could be used for farm work.

Wheel strengthened to carry heavy loads over rough ground

Peasant farmers hoeing the land

Water buffalo

Great waterways

CHINA IS DOMINATED BY TWO GREAT RIVERS, the Yellow River in northern China and the Yangzi in the south. The Yellow River flows through the rich loess soil of its surrounding northern plains. The first civilization in China grew up in these fertile lands. Over the centuries, the Yellow River often broke its banks and caused devastating floods. This tendency to flood led to the river's other name, "China's sorrow." The Yangzi River provided a water supply for rice cultivation in the warm southern climate, and its rich delta became China's main rice-growing region. In the 6th century, the Yellow and Yangzi rivers were linked by the Grand Canal, a great waterway that stretched across the Chinese empire. The canal was used to transport rice from the Yangzi delta to northern China, where the imperial capital was situated.

A STRONG ELEMENT
According to ancient Chinese philosophy, there were two natural forces – the yin and the yang. In nature, these forces existed in a delicate state of balance. The Chinese believed the disruption of this balance by humans caused natural disasters such as floods. Therefore Chinese engineers were careful not to disturb the natural courses of rivers. In the painting above, a boy is being taught about the yin and the yang, which are symbolized by the circular sign on the scroll.

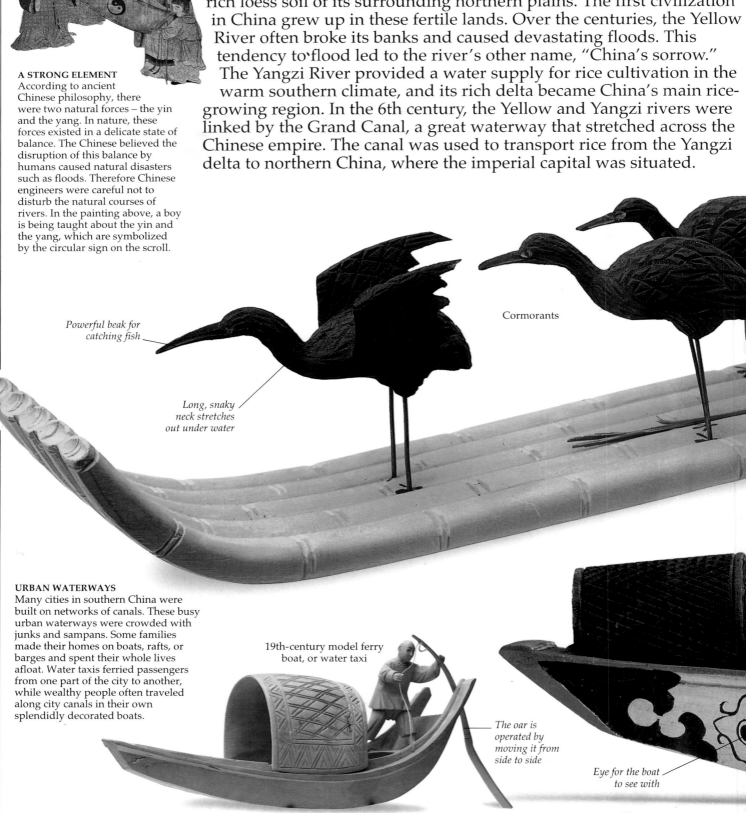

Cormorants

Powerful beak for catching fish

Long, snaky neck stretches out under water

URBAN WATERWAYS
Many cities in southern China were built on networks of canals. These busy urban waterways were crowded with junks and sampans. Some families made their homes on boats, rafts, or barges and spent their whole lives afloat. Water taxis ferried passengers from one part of the city to another, while wealthy people often traveled along city canals in their own splendidly decorated boats.

19th-century model ferry boat, or water taxi

The oar is operated by moving it from side to side

Eye for the boat to see with

THE GRAND CANAL

The Grand Canal was built by the Sui emperor Yang Di (569–618) to transport grain-tax and soldiers around his empire. It ran from Hangzhou near the Yangzi River in the south, via Luoyang near the Yellow River, to Beijing in the north, covering a distance of 1,500 miles (2,500 kilometers). This great waterway was perfected by the Ming engineer Song Li in 1411.

18th-century painting of Yang Di opening the Grand Canal

Small ferry used for carrying passengers across a river or canal

FISHING BIRDS

Some fishermen used captive cormorants, long-necked diving birds, to catch their fish. The cormorants wore rings around their necks (not shown here) to prevent them from swallowing their catch. They were also tied to the fisherman's boat so that they could be pulled back on board once they had caught a fish.

Half of the oar is missing

19th-century model fishing raft

Basket for storing fish

Flat-bottomed wooden raft

Roofing of mats

THE SIMPLE SAMPAN

The most common craft on China's waterways were simple boats called sampans, which means "three planks." Although there were many different types of sampan, the basic, flat-bottomed design remained the same for centuries.

Boat propelled by a single oar

Decorated model sampan, 19th century

Within the city walls

Circular end-tile

Lookout

KEEPING A LOOKOUT
This pottery model of a watchtower dates from the Han dynasty. Watchtowers were common in Chinese towns and cities, because the authorities kept a strict eye on the inhabitants.

THE LANDSCAPE OF IMPERIAL CHINA was dotted with walled towns and cities. These enclosed urban communities were centers of government and the power of the authorities was reinforced by town planning. Towns and cities were traditionally built on a grid system and divided into sections called wards. Each ward was surrounded by walls with gates that were locked every evening. Drums sounded from a central tower to warn inhabitants when the gates were closing, and often visiting friends or relatives would have to stay overnight. In general, wealthy people and government officials lived at one end of a town or city and the poor at the other. Markets were usually situated along one of the main streets. In the later years of the Chinese empire, towns and cities were built on a less rigid structure. However, citizens were always firmly under the control of the authorities. A French resident of 18th-century Beijing reported: "The police know all that is going on, even inside the palaces of the princes. They keep exact registers of the inhabitants of every house."

COUNTING THE COST
Towns and cities were centers for trade and commerce. Local peasant farmers brought their produce to market, and also their grain-tax to be collected by officials. Large transactions may have been carried out with the aid of an abacus. The exact origin of this helpful calculating device is unknown, but it was certainly in common use by the Ming dynasty.

ON THE TILES
Traditional Chinese buildings were protected by heavy, overhanging tile roofs. In Chinese belief, a roof was a safeguard against bad spirits as well as harsh weather. Roof tiles were often decorated with symbols and inscriptions to ward off evil influences.

The dragon is a good luck symbol

Pottery roof tiles, Ming dynasty

DRUMMING UP TRADE
This pellet-drum was used to attract customers. Street vendors had their own sounds to announce their presence and advertise their wares.

Cup for ladling out food

STREET TRADE
This man is selling food. Hawkers wandered the streets of every Chinese town or city selling cooked and uncooked foods. The main streets were lined with market stalls that sold all kinds of produce. People could buy special dishes from stallholders to take home for family meals.

A pellet-drum was held in the hand and twirled from side to side

Pottery roof ornament from a palace roof, Ming dynasty

ROOF GUARDIAN
This yellow pottery beast was placed at the end of a roof ridge. Mythical beasts like this were intended to act as guardians. Official buildings and the houses of wealthy people were often highly ornamented with decorated tiles and pottery figures.

Yellow roof tiles were used on important buildings

Classical pagoda

Platform

Overhanging tile roof

Traditional Chinese buildings, Ming dynasty

TRADITIONAL ARCHITECTURE
Chinese buildings were raised above the damp ground on platforms of rammed earth, brick, or stone. Their heavy, overhanging roofs were supported by a structure of sturdy wooden beams, which allowed for movement in an earthquake.

CITY WALL
This European engraving shows the strong walls surrounding a city. Traditionally the walls of towns and cities were built in a square shape, which symbolized the four corners of the Earth. It was important for the Chinese to feel that they were in tune with nature. The site for a new town or city was carefully chosen using cosmological calculations to make sure that its position was a favorable one.

Pottery roof tiles, Ming dynasty

At home

In most Chinese homes, three generations of the same family lived under one roof. Families followed strict codes of conduct, which were reflected in the layout of their houses. A traditional home was divided into different sections by courtyards. The main gate led into an outer courtyard in which traders were received. Rooms along the sides of the outer courtyard were used for housing guests, and they often contained a library as well. An inner courtyard was reserved for the family. The head of the household, usually the grandfather, lived with his wife and children in the main building, with side rooms allocated to close relatives. Behind the main building were the kitchens and rooms for servants. Some houses were surrounded by gardens, which were enclosed within an outer wall.

Dragon head

SPECIAL ADVICE
Families used divination sticks like these to seek advice from their ancestors on family matters. They were kept with the ancestral tablets in the household shrine, where the family paid respects to their ancestors on special days of the year.

The phoenix, or fong, *is a mythical bird that symbolizes good luck*

Detail from pillow decoration

SIMPLE COMFORTS
Poorer Chinese people lived simply in their homes. They slept on rush mats and rested their heads on pillows made of wood or pottery.

Pottery pillow, 12th–13th century

Stoneware pillow, 12th–13th century

Son kneels before his father

PAYING RESPECTS
Family life in China was governed by strict rules. Confucius taught that children should respect and obey their parents, and it was written in law that a wife must be obedient to her husband. Although this sounds harsh, most Chinese families shared mutual affection and respect. This 12th-century painting shows a son, along with his wife and family, paying respects to his father.

Detail from pillow decoration

Weeping bride

LOSING A DAUGHTER
The painting on this pillow probably depicts a wedding procession. The bride is weeping because she was expected to shed tears of sorrow on leaving her own family and tears of joy on joining the family of her husband. A single girl had to obey her father; when she married, she had to obey her husband and her new parents-in-law.

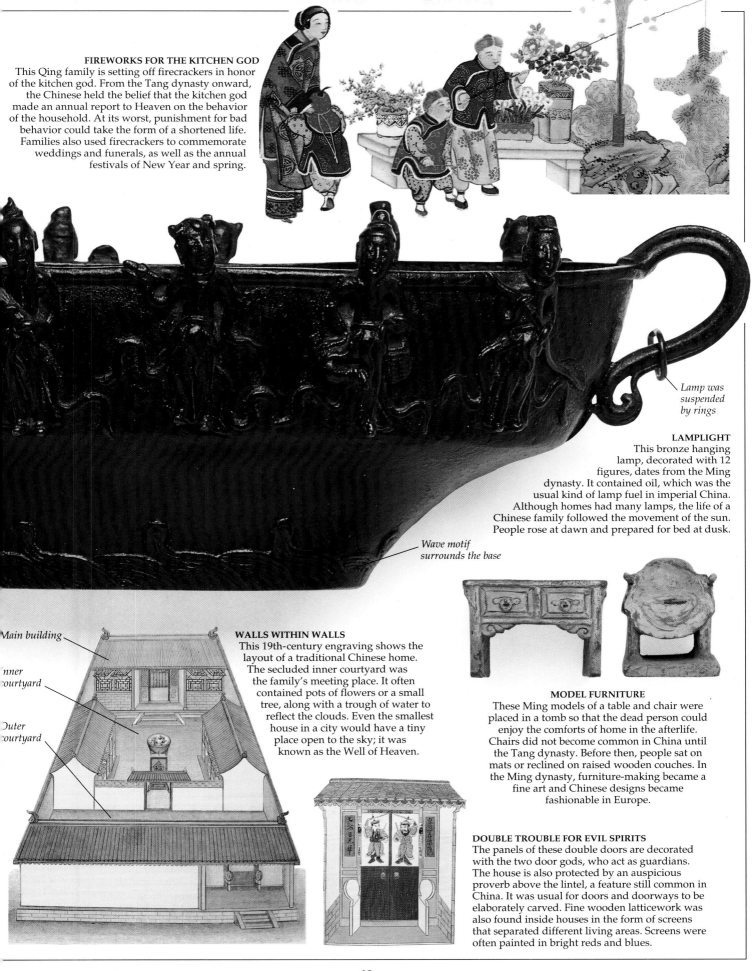

FIREWORKS FOR THE KITCHEN GOD
This Qing family is setting off firecrackers in honor of the kitchen god. From the Tang dynasty onward, the Chinese held the belief that the kitchen god made an annual report to Heaven on the behavior of the household. At its worst, punishment for bad behavior could take the form of a shortened life. Families also used firecrackers to commemorate weddings and funerals, as well as the annual festivals of New Year and spring.

Lamp was suspended by rings

LAMPLIGHT
This bronze hanging lamp, decorated with 12 figures, dates from the Ming dynasty. It contained oil, which was the usual kind of lamp fuel in imperial China. Although homes had many lamps, the life of a Chinese family followed the movement of the sun. People rose at dawn and prepared for bed at dusk.

Wave motif surrounds the base

Main building

Inner courtyard

Outer courtyard

WALLS WITHIN WALLS
This 19th-century engraving shows the layout of a traditional Chinese home. The secluded inner courtyard was the family's meeting place. It often contained pots of flowers or a small tree, along with a trough of water to reflect the clouds. Even the smallest house in a city would have a tiny place open to the sky; it was known as the Well of Heaven.

MODEL FURNITURE
These Ming models of a table and chair were placed in a tomb so that the dead person could enjoy the comforts of home in the afterlife. Chairs did not become common in China until the Tang dynasty. Before then, people sat on mats or reclined on raised wooden couches. In the Ming dynasty, furniture-making became a fine art and Chinese designs became fashionable in Europe.

DOUBLE TROUBLE FOR EVIL SPIRITS
The panels of these double doors are decorated with the two door gods, who act as guardians. The house is also protected by an auspicious proverb above the lintel, a feature still common in China. It was usual for doors and doorways to be elaborately carved. Fine wooden latticework was also found inside houses in the form of screens that separated different living areas. Screens were often painted in bright reds and blues.

Food and drink

Court ladies
enjoying a banquet,
Tang dynasty

I<small>N</small> C<small>HINA, THE ART OF COOKING</small> has been celebrated since early times. Feasts formed an important part of Chinese life, and wealthy people often enjoyed elaborate banquets. In contrast, for most of the year ordinary people lived on a simple diet of beans, grains, and vegetables, with little meat. Though rice was always the favorite staple food in China, people in the northern provinces ate mainly millet and some wheat. Both rich and poor Chinese flavored their food with a wide variety of herbs and spices. To save fuel, food was chopped into small pieces and cooked quickly in an iron frying pan, or *wok*, for a few minutes only. Many foods were also steamed or stewed. Today Chinese food is enjoyed throughout the world.

A sharp knife,
the main tool of
a Chinese cook

Chopsticks

Case for
chopsticks-
and-knife set

TEA CONNOISSEURS
Tea, or *cha*, has been grown in China since the 2nd century B.C. By the Tang dynasty, tea-making had become a fine art. These Yuan-dynasty tea merchants are taking part in a tea-tasting competition. As experts, they would be able to tell apart the many delicately flavored varieties of Chinese tea.

NATURALLY PRESERVED
The Chinese preserved much of their food by drying it in the sun, and dried ingredients are common in Chinese cookery. After soaking in cold water, this dried cuttlefish can be used to flavor a stir-fried dish.

Song-dynasty tea
bowls, 12th
century

TIME FOR TEA
From Tang times, tea was sipped from small bowls that rested on lacquer bowl stands. Boiled water was poured from a ewer onto powdered tea in a bowl. In the 13th century people began to steep loose leaves in hot water, and the teapot came into use. Many leaf varieties are grown, but the drying method produces three main types of tea: black (red or coppery), oolong (amber), and green (pale yellow-green). Leaves are often chopped and blended, and some teas contain flowers. The tea shown right is called gunpowder tea because its leaves are rolled into balls that resemble lead shot.

Peanuts, eaten as a tasty
snack or added to
cooked dishes

*Tea leaves
unfurl when
soaked in water*

CHOPSTICKS
In China, food is sliced into thin slivers before cooking, so people do not need to use knives to cut up their food when they are eating. Instead, the Chinese use chopsticks to pick up morsels of food from small porcelain bowls.

Porcelain bowl,
18th century

Peas,
often ground
into flour

Mung
beans, eaten as
a dessert or a
side dish

*A china bowl
preserves the
taste of food*

Soy beans,
processed into bean
curd, milk, dried sticks,
or soy sauce

Wheat, often used to
make dumplings

Bean curd, or *doufu*
(tofu), can be steamed,
boiled, or fried

Rice, used to make
wine as well as cakes
and puddings

A STAPLE DIET
Rice was grown mainly in the
southern Chinese provinces, but with
improved transportation it became the favorite
staple food throughout China. Millet and
wheat were the chief crops grown in the north,
but wheat never formed a staple part of the
Chinese diet as it did in Europe and America.
Beans were an important source of protein for
the Chinese – soy beans contain more
protein than any other plant or animal food.

THE SPICE OF LIFE
The Chinese have always relished different
tastes and flavors. Chinese cooks became
expert at blending herbs and spices to create
sweet, sour, bitter, hot, or salty tastes.
Seasoning was important to ordinary people
because much of their basic diet consisted of
quite bland food. Soy beans were fermented to
make tasty soy sauce. More delicate flavors
were derived from ingredients such as
flower petals and tangerine peel.

Star anise, a
popular spice
native to
China

Chili peppers,
traditionally
added to hot,
spicy dishes in
southwestern
China

Noodles,
made from wheat,
bean, or rice flour

Ginger, originally
used to disguise the
odor of overripe meat

Sesame seeds,
sprinkled on
both sweet and
savory foods

Dressed for best

THE CLOTHES OF RICH AND POOR Chinese were very different. Peasant farmers wore loose garments made of hemp, a rough fabric woven from plant fibers. Members of the imperial court, wealthy ladies, high-ranking officials, and scholars wore splendid robes of fine silk. This luxurious material was reserved exclusively for the use of these privileged groups. In some dynasties, rich merchants who traded in silk were forbidden from wearing it themselves, and many were punished for wearing fine silk beneath their outer garments. The supply of materials used for making clothes was protected by imperial decree. Both hemp and silk cloth were stockpiled in government storehouses in case of shortages. Toward the end of the empire, cotton became popular, but it never replaced silk as a luxury fabric.

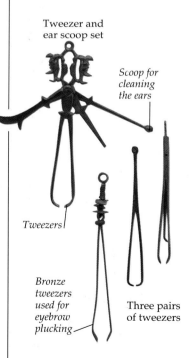

PERSONAL GROOMING
Beauty treatment was always a matter of concern for the wellborn Chinese lady. The eyebrows received special attention. They were plucked with tweezers and were usually enhanced by painting as well.

Tweezer and ear scoop set

Scoop for cleaning the ears

Tweezers

Bronze tweezers used for eyebrow plucking

Three pairs of tweezers

Luxurious vermilion dyed silk

Scoop

Jade ear scoop

Tongue scraper

Silk tassels

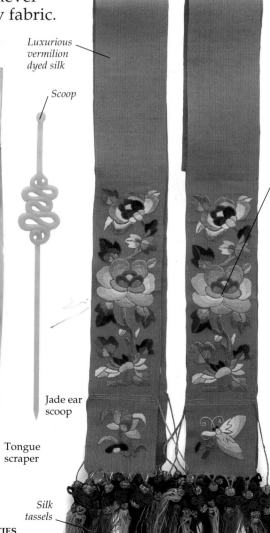

SILK TIES
These red silk ankle bands were used for binding on gaiters. The richness of the embroidery shows that they came from the wardrobe of a wealthy lady. Embroidery was common on clothes worn by both men and women of quality. Designs often included good luck symbols or mythological scenes.

The peony, often called the "king of flowers" because of its large red petals, was a popular decorative motif

The oute segment of the fa is decorated with garden scen

CARVED IVORY FAN
Fans were a favorite item of dress for both men and women in China. This expensive ivory fan is decorated with intricately carved flowers and trees. Cheaper fans were made of bamboo and paper. Their decoration could take the form of a painting or a poem.

Delicate flowers embroidered in silk thread

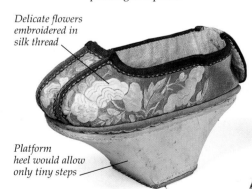

Platform heel would allow only tiny steps

PLATFORM SHOE
This delicate platform slipper belonged to a Manchu lady. The Manchus ruled China during the Qing dynasty. Unlike many Chinese women, Manchu women did not bind their feet to make them smaller. The Chinese believed that tiny, pointed feet were an essential feature of female beauty, and girls' feet were bound from early childhood. Not until 1902 did an emperor issue an order banning this painful practice.

Fine silk cloth is light to wear

Wide sleeve

Miniature roundel, or circular design

lk toggle ed to fasten e robe

he butterfly a symbol joy

he yellow tus is sacred hinese wer

FLOWING SILK ROBE
The beauty of this 19th-century silk robe indicates that it was once worn by a lady of considerable taste. It is made from a kind of silk tapestry, called *kesi*, in which the pattern is woven into the fabric. The wonderful design of flowers and butterflies is intended to create the impression of spring. Along the hem, the garment is finished with a traditional wave border.

An elaborate roundel, a design popular toward the end of the empire

The bat is an emblem of good luck

The peony represents spring

Wave border

Adornment

FOR THE CHINESE, THE WAY people dressed was never a casual matter. Personal ornaments were worn by men and women both as decoration and as a sign of rank. Through jewelry one could tell at a glance a person's position in China's rigid social hierarchy. From early times, belt hooks and plaques were the most important items of jewelry for men, while women decorated their elaborate hairstyles with beautiful hairpins and combs. In the later Chinese empire, jewelry became an important part of official costume, and the materials used to make it were regulated by law. These rules did not apply to women's jewelry. Wealthy women wore stunning pieces made of gold or silver and set with pearls, precious stones, and kingfisher feathers.

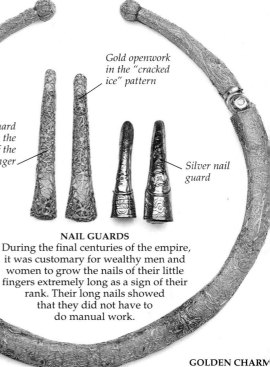

Gold openwork in the "cracked ice" pattern

Nail guard protects the long nail of the little finger

Silver nail guard

NAIL GUARDS
During the final centuries of the empire, it was customary for wealthy men and women to grow the nails of their little fingers extremely long as a sign of their rank. Their long nails showed that they did not have to do manual work.

GOLDEN CHARM
This lovely gold neckle from the Qing dynasty is decorated with lucky, or auspicious, symbols. The symbols were intended to bring the wearer good luck and to ward off evil influences. Even today Chinese jewelry has a semimagical purpose.

Garment hook shaped like a lute

Intricate inlay of turquoise and gold

Bronze belt hook inlaid with silver

The end of a belt hook fits into a ring or buckle

BY HOOK OR BY CROOK
Belt and garment hooks came into use in China in about the 4th century B.C. They were probably copied from neighboring tribes such as the Xiongnu nomads. In early China, hooks were made of bronze and were often inlaid with gold, silver, and semiprecious stones. Decorated hooks became an essential part of the wardrobe of Chinese men.

Dragon head

Cicada-shaped belt hook

Decorative dragon

BUCKLE UP
Belt hooks fastened into buckles like these, which were also highly decorated.

The end of the hook pokes through here

ARMLET
After jade, gold was the most prized material used by Chinese craftsmen. This armlet is made of solid gold coiled into a spiral. It is one of a pair that dates from the Mongol, or Yuan dynasty.

Two birds entwined

WEIGHTY MATTERS
Sleeve weights such as these were used to weigh down the long, flowing sleeves of ceremonial robes. They helped the wide sleeves to hang properly and kept them from flapping around. These two bird-shaped sleeve weights date from the Tang dynasty. They are made of bronze and decorated with bright gilding.

Bronze mirror, Han dynasty

Pair of openwork gold hairpins, Tang dynasty

PINNED IN PLACE
Chinese women paid particular attention to their hair. From early times, they wore elaborate hairstyles that were held in place with combs and hairpins. Wealthy women used beautifully decorated hairpins made of gold, silver, jade, and glass.

Group of four gold and silver hairpins, Qing dynasty

The mirror was held or suspended by a central boss, or stud

MIRROR IMAGES
By the Han dynasty, bronze mirrors were mass-produced throughout China. The Chinese believed that mirrors represented harmony within the universe. They were often decorated with cosmological signs, as is the mirror above. The reverse side was highly polished to act as a reflector.

Floral design enhanced with gilding

HAIR CARE
This impressive silver comb may have belonged to a beautiful court lady. Such women often underwent several hours of hairdressing every morning. Personal maids combed and twisted their hair into the fashionable hairstyles of the day.

Fine silver prongs

HAIR ORNAMENT
This hollow jade hair ornament fitted over a topknot and was held in place by a hairpin. Chinese women favored complex hairstyles and hair ornaments were their favorite items of jewelry.

Peony design molded on lid

Fruiting vine motif

PRECIOUS GIFTS
During the Han dynasty, the Chinese constantly fought and made peace with the fierce Xiongnu nomads who roamed the lands north of the Great Wall. Peaceful relations were celebrated with the exchange of gifts. The Chinese received decorated belt hooks, plaques, and buckles. These exotic ornaments were widely copied until they became an integral part of Chinese dress.

Griffin attacking a tiger

GILDING THE LILY
Well-to-do women enhanced their appearance with cosmetics. This delicate 18th-century cosmetic box contains tiny paint palettes in the shape of a lotus.

Bronze belt plaque, 4th–3rd century B.C.

A SIGN OF SUCCESS
Expensive belt plaques such as this one on the left were often worn by high-ranking officials as a sign of status. This elegant 14th-century plaque is made of silver and gilt.

MARTIAL JEWELRY
This gilt bronze belt plaque dates from the 3rd–1st century B.C. It is an example of the kind of belt decoration copied by the Chinese from their warlike nomadic neighbors. The bold design shows two horses fighting. Belt plaques were sewn onto the front of a belt.

Festivals and games

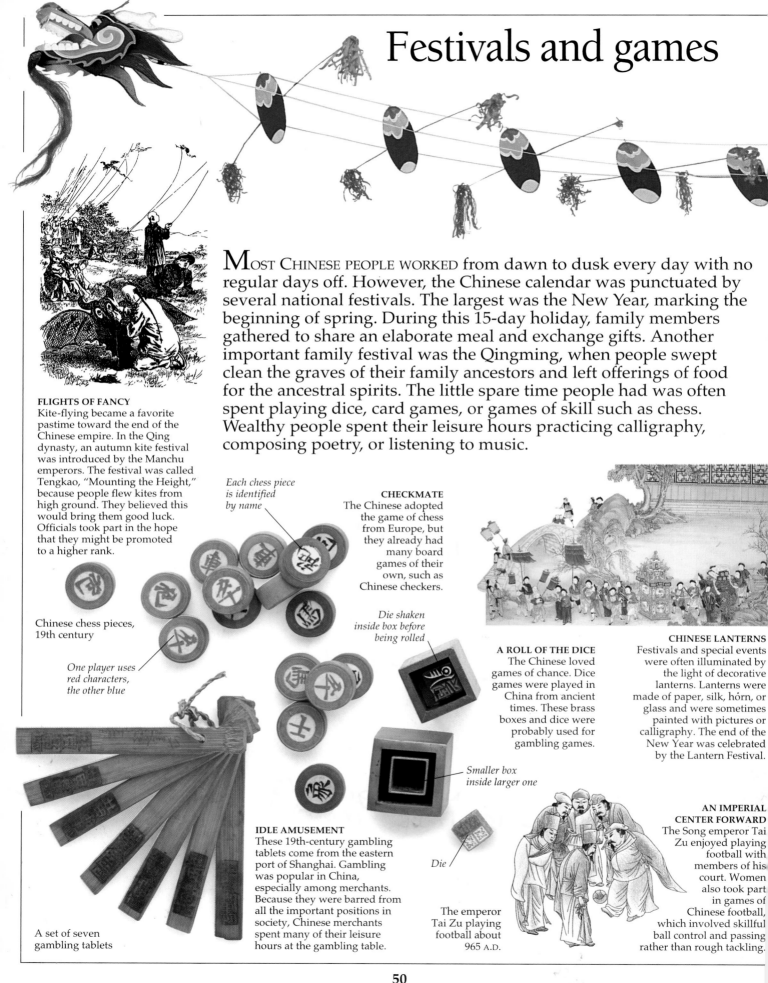

MOST CHINESE PEOPLE WORKED from dawn to dusk every day with no regular days off. However, the Chinese calendar was punctuated by several national festivals. The largest was the New Year, marking the beginning of spring. During this 15-day holiday, family members gathered to share an elaborate meal and exchange gifts. Another important family festival was the Qingming, when people swept clean the graves of their family ancestors and left offerings of food for the ancestral spirits. The little spare time people had was often spent playing dice, card games, or games of skill such as chess. Wealthy people spent their leisure hours practicing calligraphy, composing poetry, or listening to music.

FLIGHTS OF FANCY
Kite-flying became a favorite pastime toward the end of the Chinese empire. In the Qing dynasty, an autumn kite festival was introduced by the Manchu emperors. The festival was called Tengkao, "Mounting the Height," because people flew kites from high ground. They believed this would bring them good luck. Officials took part in the hope that they might be promoted to a higher rank.

Each chess piece is identified by name

CHECKMATE
The Chinese adopted the game of chess from Europe, but they already had many board games of their own, such as Chinese checkers.

Chinese chess pieces, 19th century

One player uses red characters, the other blue

Die shaken inside box before being rolled

A ROLL OF THE DICE
The Chinese loved games of chance. Dice games were played in China from ancient times. These brass boxes and dice were probably used for gambling games.

CHINESE LANTERNS
Festivals and special events were often illuminated by the light of decorative lanterns. Lanterns were made of paper, silk, horn, or glass and were sometimes painted with pictures or calligraphy. The end of the New Year was celebrated by the Lantern Festival.

Smaller box inside larger one

IDLE AMUSEMENT
These 19th-century gambling tablets come from the eastern port of Shanghai. Gambling was popular in China, especially among merchants. Because they were barred from all the important positions in society, Chinese merchants spent many of their leisure hours at the gambling table.

Die

The emperor Tai Zu playing football about 965 A.D.

A set of seven gambling tablets

AN IMPERIAL CENTER FORWARD
The Song emperor Tai Zu enjoyed playing football with members of his court. Women also took part in games of Chinese football, which involved skillful ball control and passing rather than rough tackling.

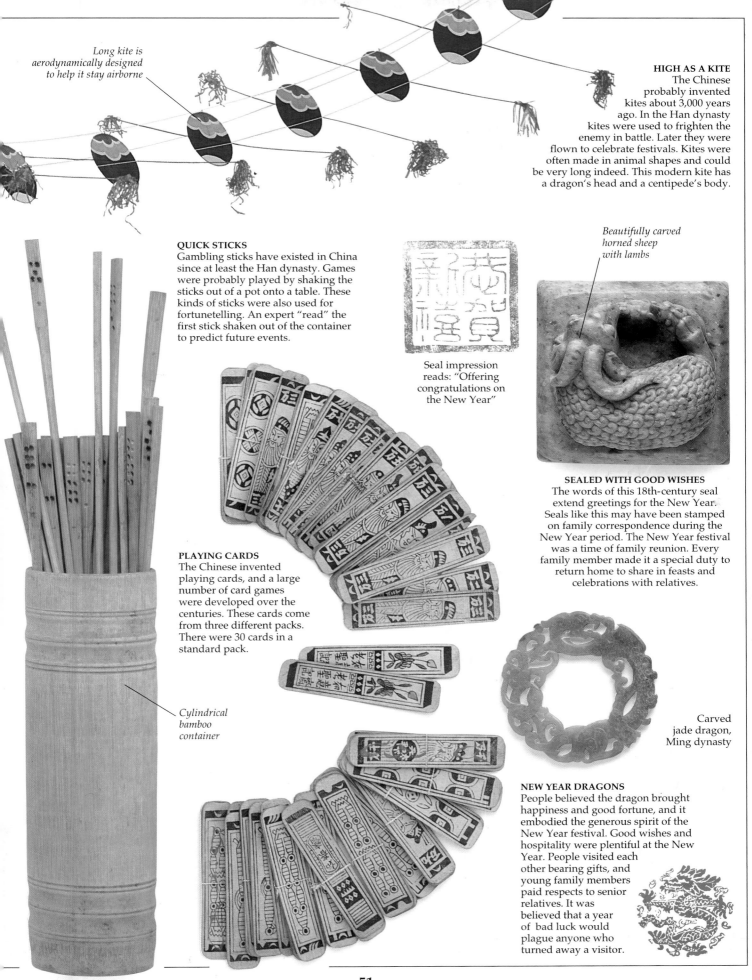

Long kite is aerodynamically designed to help it stay airborne

HIGH AS A KITE
The Chinese probably invented kites about 3,000 years ago. In the Han dynasty kites were used to frighten the enemy in battle. Later they were flown to celebrate festivals. Kites were often made in animal shapes and could be very long indeed. This modern kite has a dragon's head and a centipede's body.

QUICK STICKS
Gambling sticks have existed in China since at least the Han dynasty. Games were probably played by shaking the sticks out of a pot onto a table. These kinds of sticks were also used for fortunetelling. An expert "read" the first stick shaken out of the container to predict future events.

Seal impression reads: "Offering congratulations on the New Year"

Beautifully carved horned sheep with lambs

SEALED WITH GOOD WISHES
The words of this 18th-century seal extend greetings for the New Year. Seals like this may have been stamped on family correspondence during the New Year period. The New Year festival was a time of family reunion. Every family member made it a special duty to return home to share in feasts and celebrations with relatives.

PLAYING CARDS
The Chinese invented playing cards, and a large number of card games were developed over the centuries. These cards come from three different packs. There were 30 cards in a standard pack.

Cylindrical bamboo container

Carved jade dragon, Ming dynasty

NEW YEAR DRAGONS
People believed the dragon brought happiness and good fortune, and it embodied the generous spirit of the New Year festival. Good wishes and hospitality were plentiful at the New Year. People visited each other bearing gifts, and young family members paid respects to senior relatives. It was believed that a year of bad luck would plague anyone who turned away a visitor.

Living in harmony

IN IMPERIAL CHINA, MUSIC was thought to be an important part of civilized life. At the royal palace, the court orchestra played when the emperor received visitors or held banquets. Beautiful ceremonial music also accompanied religious rituals. Confucius thought music was almost as necessary as food. He believed that playing an instrument, singing, or listening to a suitable musical composition encouraged a sense of inner harmony. On the other hand, he thought that certain kinds of music led to rowdy or violent behavior, and he condemned these as immoral. As an unknown scholar remarked, "The greatest music is that filled with the most delicate sounds."

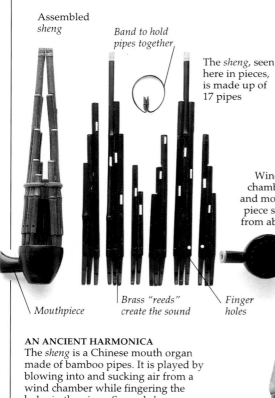

Assembled *sheng*

Band to hold pipes together

The *sheng*, seen here in pieces, is made up of 17 pipes

Wind chamber and mouth-piece seen from above

Mouthpiece

Brass "reeds" create the sound

Finger holes

AN ANCIENT HARMONICA
The *sheng* is a Chinese mouth organ made of bamboo pipes. It is played by blowing into and sucking air from a wind chamber while fingering the holes in the pipes. Several *sheng* were played together. This kind of wind instrument has been in existence in China since ancient times.

MUSIC IN THE AFTERLIFE
Since music was considered such an important part of life, models of musicians were often placed in tombs to provide entertainment in the afterlife. These elegant terra-cotta musicians and dancer were found in a Tang-dynasty tomb. The figures were once painted with bright colors.

Long, flowing sleeve

Dancer

Harp

Remnants of bright red paint on robe

Strings would have been threaded into model

Bridge

Perforations let sound out of box

MANY STRINGS ATTACHED
The *yang qin*, or "foreign zither," was a late addition to the Chinese orchestra. It was introduced into China in about the 18th century and soon became popular. The *yang qin* is played by striking the strings with a pair of delicate beaters. Its 14 strings produce a wide range of silvery notes.

Wooden beaters

Tuning tool

Tuning pegs

Lacquered board

Bridge

9th-century *qin*

Strings are plucked by hand

THE LYRICAL LUTE
The classical lute, or *qin*, is a kind of Chinese zither with seven strings. The *qin* dates back more than 2,000 years, and older designs had up to 20 strings. The music of the *qin* was greatly admired for its gentle, plaintive quality, and it was a favorite instrument in imperial China.

Mother-of-pearl disks indicate finger positions

Remnants of blue paint on headdress

Flute

Lute

COURT ORCHESTRA
Many court occasions were accompanied by music. These female musicians are playing various wind and string instruments, including the *sheng*, the flute, and the *qin*. The musician in the bottom right corner is playing another popular Chinese instrument, the drum.

Gardens of Heaven

THE CHINESE LOOKED ON GARDENS as works of art. The main elements of a garden were the same as those of a traditional landscape painting – craggy mountains and still water. These appeared in gardens as outcrops of weatherworn rock and tranquil lakes or ponds. Chinese gardens were designed to reflect nature in other ways. Trees were allowed to grow into interesting gnarled shapes, and plants and flowers were cultivated in natural-looking clumps. The garden was a place for quiet thought and spiritual refreshment. Unexpected features that inspired the imagination were prized, and graceful pavilions and bridges enhanced the impression of natural harmony. Towns and cities were planned to include secluded parks where, as a Ming garden treatise promised, the urban population could find "stillness in the midst of the city turmoil."

NATURE PERFECTED
The natural arrangement of the Chinese garden can be seen in this 19th-century painting of the palace gardens in Beijing. Visitors to these famous landscape gardens felt they were entering a natural paradise. Artificial hills and lakes, bright flowers, elegant pines, and ornamental rocks were creatively assembled to reflect the glories of nature.

Detail from purse decoration

With its sweet song, the Chinese cicada was a welcome visitor to the garden

Lotus-shaped cup carved from horn

KING OF FLOWERS
The peony symbolized spring. It was known as the "king of flowers" because of its large, red petals. Chinese gardeners planted peonies in dense clumps or along walls.

The bright, dancing butterfly was a symbol of joy

SACRED BLOSSOMS
The lotus was regarded as the supreme flower of summer. Its pale blossoms graced the tranquil lakes and pools of many Chinese parks and gardens. The lotus was seen as a symbol of purity and was sacred to both the Buddhist and Daoist religions.

Swallowtail butterfly

Peony

NATURE STUDY
This 19th-century purse is beautifully embroidered with a butterfly and a cicada. The Chinese had great respect for such tiny creatures because Buddhism taught that every living thing had a special value. Gardens were an ideal place for the study of nature. The Song emperor Hui Zong held competitions in the painting of flowers, birds, and insects in the lovely palace gardens of Kaifeng.

THE KINGDOM OF FLOWERS
The Chinese loved flowers, as the floral motif of this embroidered sleeve band shows. China was known as the "Flowery Kingdom." It is the original home of many flowers, trees, and fruits now grown throughout the world. The orange, the tea rose, the plane tree, the rhododendron, and the Chinese gooseberry, which is commonly known as the kiwi fruit, are all native Chinese plants.

FLOWER POWER
Garden plants and flowers were prized for their symbolic value as well as for their natural beauty. The winter plum blossom, for example, symbolized personal renewal, and the tough bamboo plant stood for strength and lasting friendship. These exquisite lacquer boxes from the Ming dynasty are carved with some of China's most popular flowers, including the peony and the chrysanthemum.

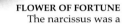

NATURALLY INSPIRED
Gardens were favorite places for literary meetings. These Ming scholars have gathered in a garden to read and write poetry. An "ink boy" prepares a supply of ink to make sure that the scholar who is about to compose verse will not have to interrupt his flow once inspiration strikes.

FRUIT OF PARADISE
The bright red fruit of the lychee tree adorned many gardens in southern China. This attractive fruit was also prized for its juicy white flesh.

LASTING BEAUTY
The chrysanthemum, flower of autumn, was esteemed for the variety and richness of its colors. Because it outlasted the frost, the chrysanthemum was adopted as the Chinese symbol for long life.

FLOWER OF FORTUNE
The narcissus was a favorite New Year flower. The opening of its delicate buds was thought to bring good luck for the year ahead.

Details from sleeve band decoration

A lovely butterfly attracted to fragrant garden flowers

The chrysanthemum was carefully cultivated in China

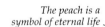

The peach is a symbol of eternal life

Arts and crafts

CHINA HAS ALWAYS BEEN RENOWNED for its exquisite arts and crafts. In imperial China, luxury goods formed the major export commodities – Chinese bronze, jade, silk, lacquer, and porcelain were prized in Asia and Europe. Although the manufacture of decorative objects involved sophisticated techniques, many were mass-produced. From the Shang dynasty onward, Chinese rulers controlled the supply of raw materials and ran government factories manned by skilled artisans who applied their crafts to different stages of the manufacturing processes.

Unlike the merchants who sold their handiwork, artisans were well thought of in China. After the scholars and the peasant farmers, artisans were considered the most important members of society. They produced tools for agriculture and weapons for the army as well as luxury items such as decorated tableware and fine silk cloth.

BEAUTIFUL BRONZE
In ancient China, bronze was made into stunning ritual vessels and weaponry. This circular fitting, which dates from Shang times, probably decorated a harness or a shield. Later, in about the 6th century B.C., the Chinese refined the process of iron casting. From then on government iron foundries produced iron and even steel in bulk.

Lead glazes run to give a swirly pattern

Underside of teacup

Mother-of-pearl inlay

Gold leaf or gold dust is applied to bronze for a bright finish

Bronze Buddha, Ming dynasty

POTS OF STYLE
China is famous for its beautiful, high-quality ceramics. This is due partly to the rich deposits of suitable clay and porcelain stone found in China. Over the centuries Chinese craftsmen developed a wide range of innovative techniques for making and decorating ceramics. One of the most famous styles was the blue-and-white porcelain manufactured in the Ming dynasty. Large amounts of this were exported to Europe from the 15th century onward. Another distinctive style was the "three-color" pottery popular in the Tang dynasty. This was decorated with three colors of lead glaze to create bold, splashy patterns, as seen on the Tang teacups above.

BURNISHED GOLD
Some of China's finest pieces of art were religious or ceremonial objects. This beautiful gilt bronze figure represents the Buddha of Immeasurable Light. Chinese craftsmen often decorated the Buddha with bright, shining gold, or gilt, to emphasize his holiness.

FIT FOR A KING
This exquisite box from the Ming dynasty is made of lacquered basketry inlaid with mother-of-pearl. It is decorated with a romantic scene showing a scholar taking leave of his friends. A lacquered finish took many days to produce and was usually highly decorated. Since lacquerware was both expensive and beautiful, it was often given as an imperial gift to neighboring rulers. In Korea and Japan Chinese lacquer was greatly admired.

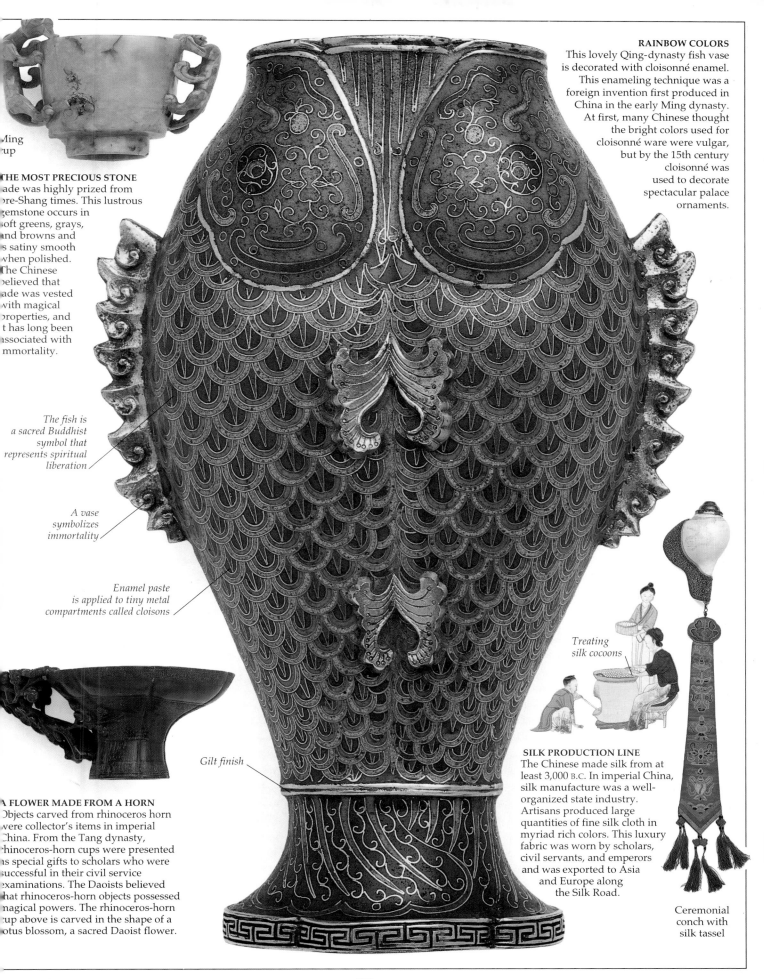

Ming cup

THE MOST PRECIOUS STONE

Jade was highly prized from pre-Shang times. This lustrous gemstone occurs in soft greens, grays, and browns and is satiny smooth when polished. The Chinese believed that jade was vested with magical properties, and it has long been associated with immortality.

The fish is a sacred Buddhist symbol that represents spiritual liberation

A vase symbolizes immortality

Enamel paste is applied to tiny metal compartments called cloisons

Gilt finish

A FLOWER MADE FROM A HORN

Objects carved from rhinoceros horn were collector's items in imperial China. From the Tang dynasty, rhinoceros-horn cups were presented as special gifts to scholars who were successful in their civil service examinations. The Daoists believed that rhinoceros-horn objects possessed magical powers. The rhinoceros-horn cup above is carved in the shape of a lotus blossom, a sacred Daoist flower.

RAINBOW COLORS

This lovely Qing-dynasty fish vase is decorated with cloisonné enamel. This enameling technique was a foreign invention first produced in China in the early Ming dynasty. At first, many Chinese thought the bright colors used for cloisonné ware were vulgar, but by the 15th century cloisonné was used to decorate spectacular palace ornaments.

Treating silk cocoons

SILK PRODUCTION LINE

The Chinese made silk from at least 3,000 B.C. In imperial China, silk manufacture was a well-organized state industry. Artisans produced large quantities of fine silk cloth in myriad rich colors. This luxury fabric was worn by scholars, civil servants, and emperors and was exported to Asia and Europe along the Silk Road.

Ceremonial conch with silk tassel

The Silk Road

TRADE FLOURISHED under the Mongol, or Yuan, dynasty. The Mongol emperors ruled China from 1279 to 1368 and permitted merchants to trade freely throughout their vast empire. They controlled the entire length of the Silk Road, a series of trade routes that ran from northern China across Asia. International trade thrived because caravans could travel without danger. Chinese merchants amassed large fortunes by exporting luxury goods such as silk, spices, teas, porcelain, and lacquerware. At home in China, the Mongols removed the usual restraints placed upon merchants. Traditionally, merchants were excluded from civil service jobs and were subject to heavy taxes. But for most of their rule, the Mongols ignored the opinions of Chinese officials, and the social position of merchants temporarily improved.

THE MONGOL CONQUEST
The Mongols came from north of the Great Wall. They were herdsmen who had expert cavalry skills, which made their army virtually unbeatable. After years of fighting, Genghis Khan (1167–1227) conquered China. By 1279, the empire was under complete Mongol control. Genghis Khan's grandson, Kublai Khan, ruled almost the whole of East Asia until his death in 1294.

Blue-and-white jar, 14th century

PORCELAIN PERFECTION
This magnificent porcelain jar from the Yuan dynasty is an example of the finely crafted ceramics that were exported to Asia and Europe. The blue-and-white style became widely popular in the Ming dynasty, which succeeded the Yuan.

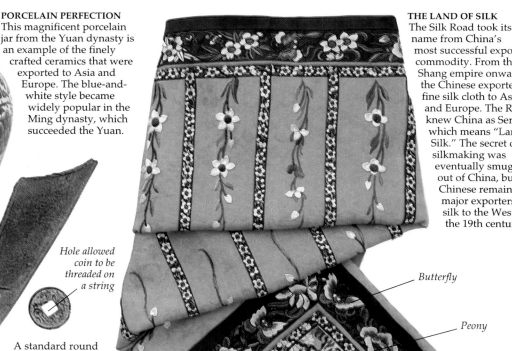

THE LAND OF SILK
The Silk Road took its name from China's most successful export commodity. From the Shang empire onward, the Chinese exported fine silk cloth to Asia and Europe. The Romans knew China as Serica, which means "Land of Silk." The secret of silkmaking was eventually smuggled out of China, but the Chinese remained the major exporters of silk to the West until the 19th century.

Butterfly

Peony

Hole allowed coin to be threaded on a string

A standard round coin introduced by the First Emperor

Knife-shaped bronze coin, c. 500 B.C.

MAKING MONEY
In ancient times, traveling merchants used silver money shaped like knives or spades. The First Emperor introduced round bronze coins, known as *cash*. They remained in use for more than 2,000 years. Paper money first appeared in the 11th century and was widely used in the Yuan dynasty.

Silver pieces, used as money throughout the Chinese empire

Money shaped like a shoe

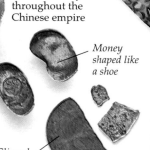

Clipped coin

Silver ingot

Standard-sized bolts of silk cloth were used as money from the Han to the Tang dynasty

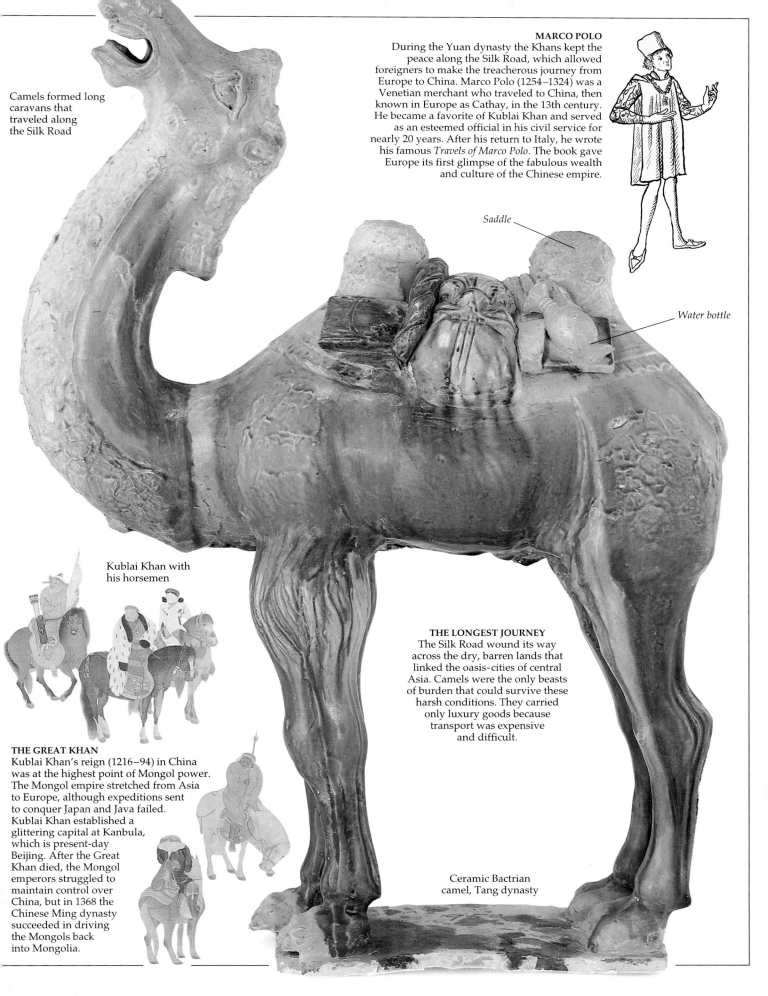

Camels formed long
caravans that
traveled along
the Silk Road

MARCO POLO
During the Yuan dynasty the Khans kept the
peace along the Silk Road, which allowed
foreigners to make the treacherous journey from
Europe to China. Marco Polo (1254–1324) was a
Venetian merchant who traveled to China, then
known in Europe as Cathay, in the 13th century.
He became a favorite of Kublai Khan and served
as an esteemed official in his civil service for
nearly 20 years. After his return to Italy, he wrote
his famous *Travels of Marco Polo*. The book gave
Europe its first glimpse of the fabulous wealth
and culture of the Chinese empire.

Saddle

Water bottle

Kublai Khan with
his horsemen

THE LONGEST JOURNEY
The Silk Road wound its way
across the dry, barren lands that
linked the oasis-cities of central
Asia. Camels were the only beasts
of burden that could survive these
harsh conditions. They carried
only luxury goods because
transport was expensive
and difficult.

THE GREAT KHAN
Kublai Khan's reign (1216–94) in China
was at the highest point of Mongol power.
The Mongol empire stretched from Asia
to Europe, although expeditions sent
to conquer Japan and Java failed.
Kublai Khan established a
glittering capital at Kanbula,
which is present-day
Beijing. After the Great
Khan died, the Mongol
emperors struggled to
maintain control over
China, but in 1368 the
Chinese Ming dynasty
succeeded in driving
the Mongols back
into Mongolia.

Ceramic Bactrian
camel, Tang dynasty

Great ocean voyages

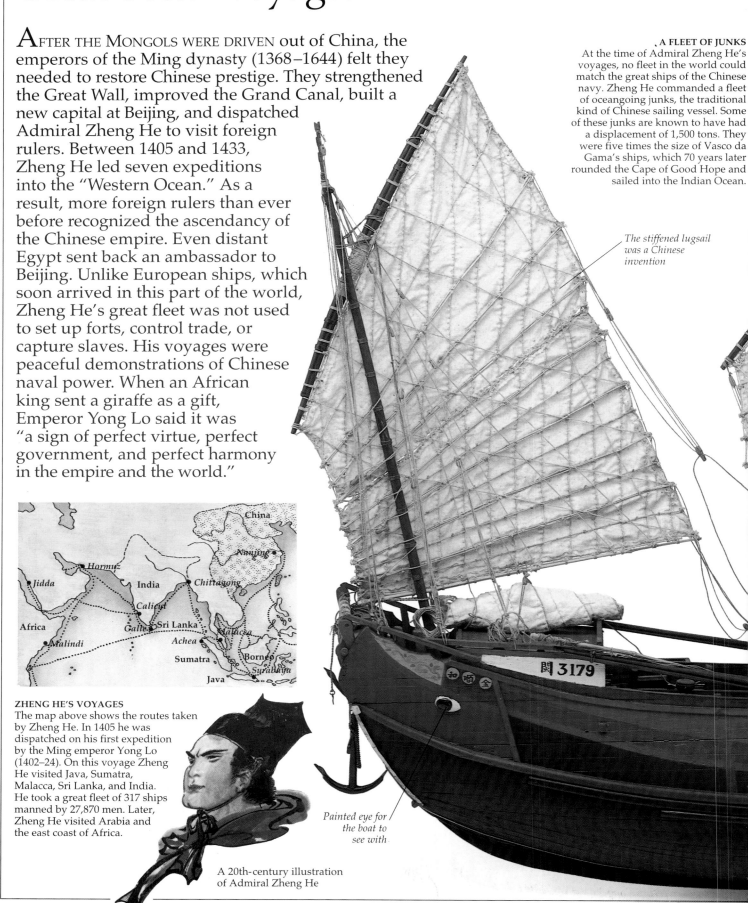

AFTER THE MONGOLS WERE DRIVEN out of China, the emperors of the Ming dynasty (1368–1644) felt they needed to restore Chinese prestige. They strengthened the Great Wall, improved the Grand Canal, built a new capital at Beijing, and dispatched Admiral Zheng He to visit foreign rulers. Between 1405 and 1433, Zheng He led seven expeditions into the "Western Ocean." As a result, more foreign rulers than ever before recognized the ascendancy of the Chinese empire. Even distant Egypt sent back an ambassador to Beijing. Unlike European ships, which soon arrived in this part of the world, Zheng He's great fleet was not used to set up forts, control trade, or capture slaves. His voyages were peaceful demonstrations of Chinese naval power. When an African king sent a giraffe as a gift, Emperor Yong Lo said it was "a sign of perfect virtue, perfect government, and perfect harmony in the empire and the world."

A FLEET OF JUNKS
At the time of Admiral Zheng He's voyages, no fleet in the world could match the great ships of the Chinese navy. Zheng He commanded a fleet of oceangoing junks, the traditional kind of Chinese sailing vessel. Some of these junks are known to have had a displacement of 1,500 tons. They were five times the size of Vasco da Gama's ships, which 70 years later rounded the Cape of Good Hope and sailed into the Indian Ocean.

The stiffened lugsail was a Chinese invention

ZHENG HE'S VOYAGES
The map above shows the routes taken by Zheng He. In 1405 he was dispatched on his first expedition by the Ming emperor Yong Lo (1402–24). On this voyage Zheng He visited Java, Sumatra, Malacca, Sri Lanka, and India. He took a great fleet of 317 ships manned by 27,870 men. Later, Zheng He visited Arabia and the east coast of Africa.

Painted eye for the boat to see with

A 20th-century illustration of Admiral Zheng He

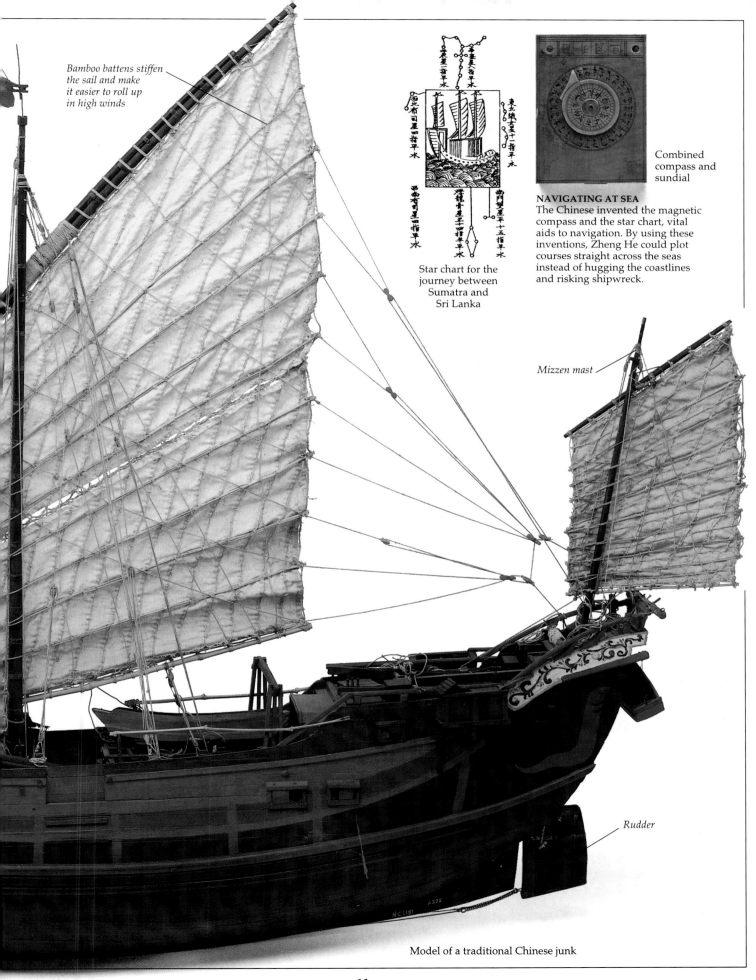

Bamboo battens stiffen the sail and make it easier to roll up in high winds

Star chart for the journey between Sumatra and Sri Lanka

Combined compass and sundial

NAVIGATING AT SEA
The Chinese invented the magnetic compass and the star chart, vital aids to navigation. By using these inventions, Zheng He could plot courses straight across the seas instead of hugging the coastlines and risking shipwreck.

Mizzen mast

Rudder

Model of a traditional Chinese junk

The end of the empire

DURING THE LAST 250 YEARS of the Chinese empire, the throne was occupied by the Manchus, a non-Chinese people from north of the Great Wall. China prospered for the first 150 years of the Manchu, or Qing, dynasty (1644–1911). The emperors Kangxi (1662–1722) and Qianlong (1735–96) were enlightened rulers who supported Chinese art and culture and maintained the imperial civil service. However, the Qing emperors feared that change might lead to a Chinese rebellion, and they clung to outdated traditions. For the first time Chinese technology fell behind other countries. Britain, France, Russia, and later Japan began to bully the vulnerable Qing empire in order to gain trade concessions. In 1839 a Chinese official in Canton tried to stop the import of opium, which British ships brought from India to exchange for tea. Britain declared war on China and secured a swift victory. This encouraged other countries to demand trade concessions and awards of territory. The Qing dynasty was unable to withstand the superior firepower of the invaders, and in 1900 an international force captured Beijing. In 1911, the Chinese overthrew their weakened Manchu rulers to set up a republic. The last Qing emperor, the infant Puyi (1906–67), was forced to step down in 1912, bringing to an end 2,000 years of imperial history.

A WISE RULER
The second Qing emperor, Kangxi, successfully secured Manchu rule in China. He was a wise emperor who respected Chinese culture. Unlike the previous foreign rulers, the Mongols, Kangxi employed Chinese scholars in the civil service. Many Chinese became loyal to the Qing dynasty.

PATRON OF THE ARTS
Kangxi's grandson Qianlong enjoyed a long and prosperous reign. He admired Chinese art, and it flourished under his patronage. Qianlong filled the imperial palace with a magnificent collection of paintings and artifacts, such as this beautiful elephant.

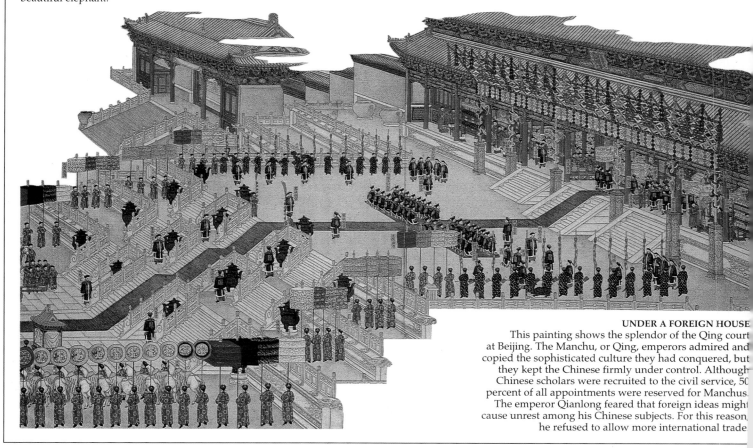

UNDER A FOREIGN HOUSE
This painting shows the splendor of the Qing court at Beijing. The Manchu, or Qing, emperors admired and copied the sophisticated culture they had conquered, but they kept the Chinese firmly under control. Although Chinese scholars were recruited to the civil service, 50 percent of all appointments were reserved for Manchus. The emperor Qianlong feared that foreign ideas might cause unrest among his Chinese subjects. For this reason, he refused to allow more international trade

xer rebels

THE BOXER REBELLION
1900, the Boxers, an
ti-foreign society in
rthern China, destroyed
ported goods and
acked Christian
ssions. An international
rce suppressed the uprising
d occupied Beijing. It was the
st straw for the Chinese empire.

BY FAIR MEANS OR FOUL
his priceless scepter was presented to
the emperor Qianlong by the French.
In the final years of the empire, there
as intense rivalry between European
powers to become the dominant
nfluence in China. France later seized
Vietnam, Laos, and Cambodia, which
were ancient Chinese allies.

*The top of the
scepter is made
in the shape of
a sacred
fungus*

*Scepter
studded with
precious jewels*

THE OPIUM WARS
1839, commissioner Li Zexu tried to
op the British from trading in opium
the port of Canton. Britain sent
nboats to support the opium traders,
d easily defeated the Chinese, as seen
ove. The British forced China to open
ur more ports to foreign trade and
give Hong Kong to Britain. This
s the beginning of the end. Soon
ina had to open ten more ports
d give territory away to France,
ssia, and other foreign powers.

DEADLY TRADE
Opium was a drug used in China, but the
Qing emperors banned its import when
the British began to sell it in vast
quantities. The British traded
specially grown Indian
opium for tea and other
prized Chinese exports
because the Chinese
were uninterested in
British goods.

19th-century
opium pipe

Qing good wishes
symbols

THE LAST EMPEROR
The last Qing emperor Puyi
(1909–1912) was placed on the
throne at the age of three. Only
three years later, revolutionaries
established a republican
government and forced him to
abdicate. Puyi was allowed to
remain in the Forbidden City
with his attendants, but
conditions worsened until he
fled to a Japanese colony in
1924. When the Japanese
invaded Manchuria in 1931,
Puyi was made emperor of
their puppet state, renamed
Manchukuo. After the war, Puyi
was imprisoned in China. Freed
in 1959, he spent his last years in
Beijing in a garden workshop.

Did you know?

AMAZING FACTS

Chinese acrobats have performed dazzling feats of skill and daring for more than 2,500 years. Tightrope walking, juggling with both hands and feet, human pagodas, and conjuring acts have been traced back as far as the Han dynasty.

The earliest acrobats used everyday objects such as tables, chairs, jars, plates, and bowls in their routines.

Dogs resembling the wrinkly Chinese shar-pei dog have been found in ancient paintings and statues dating back to the Han dynasty. These dogs were a common fixture on Chinese farms for hundreds of years, serving as guard dogs and herders. Their natural scowling expression was thought to deter bandits and thieves, and their distinctive blue-black tongue was believed to ward off evil spirits.

Shar-pei

Chinese people have been using chopsticks to eat food for about 5,000 years. Historians think that as the Chinese population grew, people had to conserve cooking fuel by chopping food into small pieces before cooking it, so that it cooked quickly. These bite-sized foods eliminated the need for knives at the dinner table. Chopsticks are usually made from bamboo, although they may also be made from other woods, plastic, porcelain, animal bone, ivory, coral, jade, or metal. Emperors and aristocrats preferred to use silver chopsticks, since they thought that silver would change color if it came into contact with any poison.

The earliest examples of Chinese writing are the inscriptions on the oracle bones made in the late Shang period (c. 1200 BCE). These artifacts were discovered by accident. In 1899, a Beijing man suffering from an illness was prescribed a remedy containing "dragon bones," or animal fossils, widely used in Chinese medicine. He noticed some carved patterns on the bones that looked like writing. Scholars later concluded that these carvings were written records dating back about 3,000 years.

Chopsticks

Chinese astrology has been practiced since 550 BCE. According to Chinese legend, the order of the twelve astrological signs was determined by Buddha. The Buddha invited all the animals in the kingdom to gather for a meeting, but only 12 arrived: rat, ox, tiger, cat, dragon, snake, horse, goat, monkey, rooster, dog, and pig. To honor them, Buddha gave each animal a year of its own, bestowing the nature and characteristics of each animal to people born in that animal's year.

Monkey

During the Han Dynasty, people in the upper classes seemed to put everything they might possibly need in the afterlife in their tombs. A few of a dead person's actual belongings were buried in the tomb, and miniature clay models were made of everything else. Typical models included horses and other farm animals, grain silos, servants, household goods, as well as small models of their above-ground homes.

Tomb animal

There was a flourishing of the arts in the Tang Dynasty. Huge orchestras with as many as 700 instruments performed at the Imperial Court. Some people preferred Bird Concerts. Bird lovers typically gathered together once a week in the mornings, bringing their caged friends with them to "sing" for the assembled crowds.

According to ancient Chinese legends, silk was discovered in 3,000 BCE by Lady Xi Ling Shi, wife of the Emperor Huang Di. A silkworm cocoon accidentally dropped into her hot tea. Fine threads from the cocoon unraveled in the hot water, and silk was discovered. The Chinese fiercely guarded the secrets of silkmaking; anyone who smuggled silk worm eggs or cocoons outside of China was punished by death.

The Chinese lantern is an important symbol of long life and a supreme totem of good luck. Originating as far back as 250 BCE, the basic lantern has not changed. The sleeve or frame that surrounds the candle is assembled from bamboo or redwood. Thin or oiled paper, gauze, or silk, in the sacred shade of vermillion red covers the frame. The rounded shape is considered lucky because it resembles money. Lanterns were once symbols of a family's wealth. The richest families had lanterns so large, it required several people with poles to hoist them into place.

In ancient China, simple firecrackers were made by roasting bamboo to produce a loud cracking sound (similar to popping corn). This noise was thought to frighten evil spirits away. The discovery of gunpowder brought much more bang to Chinese fireworks, which became an important part of any celebration.

In the Tang Dynasty, anyone with an education was expected to greet as well as say good-bye to another person in poetic verse, composed on the spot. In fact, every social occasion called for a poem, and poetry contests were very popular. Occasionally a few poets achieved national fame by having verses they composed transformed into popular songs by courtesans and entertainers.

Giant pandas date back two to three million years. The early Chinese emperors kept pandas because they were believed to ward off evil spirits, as well as natural disasters. They were also considered a symbol of might and bravery.

Pandas live almost entirely on bamboo.

Giant panda

QUESTIONS AND ANSWERS

Q What is the history of the Great Wall of China?

A In ancient times, there were many smaller walls protecting China. During the 3rd century BCE, a unified wall was built to deter raiding tribes from modern-day Mongolia and Manchuria. Workers were pulled in from all over China; many of them died during the construction period. The present-day Wall was built near the same site, mainly during the Ming dynasty (1368–1644). The Great Wall winds along the southern edge of the Mongolian plain, across deserts, grasslands, mountains, and plateaus, for an astonishing 1,500 miles (2,414 km). Built entirely by hand, it averages 25 feet (7.6 m) high and is 15 to 30 feet (4.6–9.1 m) thick at its base, tapering to a thinner top. Since 1949, two sections of the wall near Beijing have been reconstructed and are currently open to visitors.

The Great Wall of China

Q When were the Terracotta Warriors and Horses discovered?

A In 1974, a group of farmers digging for a well in the Shaanxi province uncovered some bits of very old pottery. This drew the immediate attention of archeologists, because the pottery fragments were so close to the unexcavated tomb of the First Emperor. Once experts had established that these artifacts were associated with the Qin Dynsasty, they arrived in droves. What they found became one of the most astonishing archeological excavations of the 20th century: the Terracotta Warriors and Horses. The tomb itself, rumored to contain rare gems and other treasures, has still not been excavated.

The terracotta warriors

Q When and why was the Grand Canal constructed?

A The Grand Canal, the world's oldest and longest canal, is 1,114 miles (1,795 km) long, with 24 locks and around 60 bridges. The canal was built as a commercial waterway to connect the "rice bowl" agricultural regions in the south with the dry northern plains. The oldest section, linking the Yangtze and Huang He Rivers, was built in the 4th and 5th centuries BCE. By the mid-19th century, the canal had fallen into disrepair, but the government dredged, repaired, and modernized the system in the early 1960s. Today, tourists can take boat trips up and down the canal.

Boats on the Grand Canal

Q What is China's Forbidden City? Who lived there?

A The Imperial Palace in the heart of Beijing was the residence of emperors for nearly 500 years. Popularly known as the Forbidden City, it was built in the Ming Dynasty between 1406 and 1420. This palatial complex is surrounded by 10-foot (3-m) high walls, and a deep moat. Its buildings represent the largest and best-preserved examples of Chinese traditional architecture in existence. The Outer Court was the seat of government and the site of important ceremonies, while the Inner Court was the residential area for the emperor and the imperial household.

Q What is the Summer Palace? Who created it, and why?

A Located just northwest of Beijing, the Summer Palace is the largest imperial garden in the world and an incredible example of classical Chinese gardening and architecture. Construction began in 1750 as a gift for the emperor's mother, and took 15 years to complete. The park is a vast landscape of hills and water, dotted with temples. Tourists can now enjoy what was once the private retreat of the imperial family.

Q What is the Shaolin Temple? Why is it important?

A Probably the most famous temple in China, the Shaolin Temple is renowned for its role in the development of both Chinese Buddhism and the martial arts. The temple was established in 495 in the Songshan Mountains to house Batuo, a celebrated Indian monk. In 537, another monk, Bodhidharma, settled in this temple. Legend has it that after meditating in a cave for nine years, he created a form of primitive boxing that became known as kung fu. After a tiny army of Shaolin monks scored an impressive defeat using kung fu, the temple became a thriving center for Chinese kung fu masters.

Record Breakers

TOTAL NUMBER OF EMPERORS IN ANCIENT CHINA
157, over a period of more than 2,000 years

FIRST EMPEROR
Ying Zheng, who gave himself the title Qin Shi Huangdi, was the first to rule all of China.

OLDEST EMPEROR
Emperor Wudi died at age 70, after ruling for an incredible 54 years.

ONLY EMPRESS
Empress Wu Zetian, the only female to rule as emperor, served from 690 to 705.

LONGEST REIGN
Kangxi ruled from 1661 to 1772.

SHORTEST REIGN
Taichang only ruled for a month, in 1620.

Timeline

THE CHINESE PEOPLE HAVE SHARED A COMMON culture longer than any other group of people. Dynasties were launched and overturned, emperors rose to power or were crushed in defeat, but the basic system of rule established in 221 BCE survived until 1912. In addition, the Chinese people have maintained their cultural identity throughout their tumultuous history by means of a stable social structure and a 4,000-year-old writing system. Here is a timeline to key events.

Neolithic Chinese jar

Animal-face handles, Han Dynasty

c. 10,000 BCE

The Early Neolithic period begins in China. As in other parts of the world, Neolithic settlements grew up along the main river systems. In China, the dominant rivers are the Yellow River in central and northern China, and the Yangtze in southern and eastern China.

c. 5000 BCE

Around this time, there were farming villages along the Yellow River valleys. People used polished stone tools, kept pigs and dogs, and grew millet, wheat, and barley. They made pottery jars to store their food, formed by stacking coils of clay into the desired shape and smoothing the surfaces with paddles. The pottery was decorated with red and black pigments, featuring images of plants, animals, and humans. Each village probably had a cluster of houses around a large central building for meetings, and a public cemetery behind the houses.

c. 4500 BCE

In this era early rice farmers built houses on stilts near the Yangtze River. Their pottery differed in shape from that of their northern neighbors, and included tripod-shaped pottery. They later developed a potter's wheel. These people made beautiful carvings on stone, bones, and especially jade—a very difficult and time-consuming substance to work with due to its hardness.

Silk tomb draping

c. 3000 BCE

The Bronze Age begins in China. In contrast to the European Bronze Age, the Chinese did not make bronze farming tools. Instead, they made elaborate bronze items for use in religious ceremonies.

Jade tortoise

c. 1650–1027 BCE

Shang Dynasty establishes its rule in the Central Plains. The Shang built walled towns and cities, palaces, royal tombs, and workshops for making bronze objects. Many Shang bronzes feature a distinctive two-eyed mask design called the taotie (monster face). Shang artisans were also excellent jade carvers. The first Chinese writing probably emerged during this time.

1027–256 BCE

Zhou Dynasty begins after the Shang are defeated in battle. The Zhou king divided up the land into huge estates. He gives control of these estates, as well as chariots, textiles, and slaves, to his relatives. These lords rule over the peasants and slaves, who work the land. The Zhou reign longer that any other dynasty.

481–221 BCE

Warring States period begins as the kings and lords of the Zhou begin to lose control of the country. The lords turn on each other in an attempt to gain land, staging enormous battles in which hundreds of thousands of warriors lose their lives. Early Chinese scholars react to this situation by creating new ways of thinking about the world, which we now call philosophy.

c. 400 BCE

The earliest extant paintings on silk date to this time.

551 BCE

Chinese philosopher Confucius is born. During his lifetime, he has many rivals, but his teachings later become the basis for the state religion of China and are followed by every Chinese official.

Confucius statue

221–207 BCE

Qin Dynasty (pronounced "chin," thus providing the Western name for China) begins, when the Qin state in the northwest of China unites the whole country. The king of Qin becomes the First Emperor of China. He builds lavish palaces and erects stone tablets praising his achievements. To strengthen his rule, he orders that all works of literature and philosophy be burned, and 500 scholars are buried alive. Under this dynasty, the Chinese script, currency, and system of measurements are standardized. The emperor also creates the Great Wall of China (in part from existing walls) to protect his empire, and an army of terracotta soldiers to protect him in the afterlife.

207 BCE–CE 220

Han Dynasty begins after a peasant uprising overthrows the Qin Dynasty shortly after the death of the First Emperor. The Han establish a civil service that will help to govern China's population for the next 2,000 years. The western Han capital, Chang'an, is a huge urban center with palaces, government buildings, houses, and markets, and is one of the two largest cities in the ancient world (Rome being the other). Agriculture and industry develop rapidly during this period, and ox plows and iron tools are in widespread use. Poetry, literature, and philosophy flourish at this time.

138 BCE

Emperor Wudi sends an official named Zhang Qian on a trip to central Asia to seek allies (on an earlier trip, Qian had been captured and held hostage by Huns). Qian is the first person to record anything about central Asia and its people, and trade between central Asia and China along the Silk Road increases dramatically.

c. CE 100

The earliest known example of hemp paper with Chinese writing on it dates to around this time.

CE 221–589

Period of disunity as the Han dynasty is under pressure from rebels. People rise up against the Han Dynasty, eventually bringing about its collapse. During this troubled time, the faith known as Buddhism takes hold in China. Paper, probably invented in the second century BCE, is now in widespread use as methods of paper-making have improved.

CE 589–618

Sui Dynasty reunites northern and southern China, and a period of prosperity and growing influence in the world begins. The Great Wall of China is repaired and expanded, and the Grand Canal linking the Yangtze and Yellow rivers is dug. The opening of this waterway strengthens trade and communication links around the empire.

CE 618–907

Tang Dynasty rules during what is known as the Golden Age of Chinese history. In the early years of the Tang, nomadic tribes in the north are subdued, so there is peace and safety along the trade routes. Men with merit—but without family connections—are finally allowed to join the government. The population grows and both agriculture and textile production increase. Chinese art and literature flourishes during this dynasty, as exemplified by the poets Li Bai and Du Fu, the painter Wu Daozi, and the poet/painter Wang Wei.

c. CE 700

The Tang capital city of Chang'an is now the world's largest and richest city. It is surrounded by a wall with twelve ornate gateways, and contains a huge palace and garden. Merchants from all over the world flock to the city to buy and sell goods. An early banking system is established to make business transactions easier.

c. CE 750

Drinking tea as a leisure activity becomes popular. In earlier times, tea was used chiefly as a medicine.

c. CE 868

The technique of woodblock printing is perfected. The earliest known printed book, a Buddhist text called the Diamond Sutra, is made in China using woodblock printing.

CE 907–960

Five Dynasties period begins as a peasant rebellion brings down the Tang dynasty. China is divided into north and south. A number of short-lived kingdoms spring up in the north, while the south is divided into small states.

CE 960–1279

Song Dynasty emerges to reunite China in an era of great social and economic change. Metalwork, lacquer, textiles, and other luxury goods are produced for domestic use and trade. Fine porcelain and green-glazed celadon wares are particularly important traded goods. Printing and paper-making also develop quickly, and artists paint enormous landscapes. Paper money is also invented during this era.

c. 1020

Song government encourages the spread of schools and provides support for them across China.

c. 1041

Bi Sheng invents movable type for printing. He makes a separate block for each character out of clay. The blocks can be arranged for printing and then reused.

c. 1044

The earliest formula for making gunpowder is recorded.

c. 1050

Printed books are in widespread use across China. Books and paper are also exported to other lands along trade routes.

c. 1088

Han Gonglian designs the first water-driven astronomical clock. It takes three years to construct this elaborate device, complete with 200 wooden puppets that beat drums.

Diamond Sutra scroll

c. 1200

Genghis Khan unites several nomadic tribes to establish the Mongol empire.

Paper-making mold

c. 1271

Marco Polo, the son of a merchant from Venice, Italy, arrives in China. He remains there for more than 20 years. On his return, he dazzles Europeans with reports of what he has seen in China.

1279–1368

Yuan Dynasty established after Kublai Khan (Genghis Khan's grandson) leads the Mongolian army into battle against the Song Dynasty and wins. The Mongols, now in control of the entire Silk Road, focus on international trading. Many Europeans begin to make their way to China, taking Chinese innovations and inventions back to the West.

1368–1644

Ming Dynasty begins as the Chinese push out the Mongols. This is the last Chinese dynasty. Ming emperors build most of what we now see of the Great Wall, and improve the Grand Canal. The Ming Dynasty is famous for its beautiful arts and crafts, especially blue and white ceramic wares.

Ming vase

1405–1433

Chinese explorer Zheng He makes his seven voyages of discovery. His travels take him to Southeast Asia, India, the Persian Gulf, and East Africa. His fleet is the largest in the world at the time.

c. 1406

Construction begins on the Forbidden City, which will remain the home to China's emperors until the end of the imperial era.

1644–1912

Qing Dynasty (led by the Manchu, a semi-nomadic people from northeast of the Great Wall) capture the Ming state. For the first time, Chinese technology lags behind the rest of the world, as the Qing cling to outdated traditions. Pressure from foreign countries to allow trading within China builds; after the Opium Wars (1839 and 1856) China is forced to concede both trading rights and territory.

1912

The Chinese republic is established and the last emperor, Puyi, steps down. He was allowed to remain in the Forbidden City until 1924.

Puyi, c. 1940

Find out more

IF YOU ARE EVER LUCKY ENOUGH TO JOURNEY TO CHINA, you will be able to visit some of the incredible places in this book and explore the rich history of imperial China. But you may not have to travel that far to find out more about Chinese history. Most large museums contain stunning examples of Chinese artifacts, from tools to textiles. A visit to your local Chinatown will give you a taste of Chinese culture, especially if you stop for a meal. You can also explore the cultural history of China by attending an arts event.

WOK AND ROLL
The art of cooking has been celebrated in China since ancient times. The once-exotic spices, herbs, and vegetables that have been found in Chinese kitchens for centuries are now easy to buy almost anywhere. Cooking up a delicious stir-fried meal in a Chinese wok is fun, fast, and healthy. Sign up for a Chinese cooking class, or look for tasty recipes on the Internet.

DOWN TO CHINATOWN
If there is a city in your area with a Chinatown, a stroll through its streets can be a fun way to find out more about Chinese culture. Peer inside a traditional Chinese medicine shop, explore the busy open-air markets, and stop for a bite to eat. Plan your visit to coincide with one of the major Chinese festivals: Lunar New Year, the Autumn Moon Festival, the Winter Solstice Lantern Procession, and the Dragon Boat festival are celebrated with fairs, parades, storytelling, crafts, special foods, and fireworks.

Dragon dancers hoist a colorful silk dragon in a festival parade.

SEE CHINESE ACROBATS
Chinese acrobatics has evolved into a leading art form over thousands of years. Attend a performance, and you will see why these performers were the favorites of emperors and commoners alike. It takes years of training and discipline for acrobats to reach this level of skill. You will be astounded by their daring and sheer precision. Check your newspaper entertainment listings or use the Internet to locate a performance.

USEFUL WEB SITES

www.ancientchina.co.uk/menu.html
The British Museum's guide to ancient China

www.historyforkids.org/learn/china/
A cool learning site for children dedicated to ancient and Medieval China, with plenty of activities

www.asianart.com
A guide to the art of ancient China and Asia

www.condensedchina.com
A beginner's introduction to China's history

TRY AN ANCIENT CHINESE CRAFT

Anyone can put pen to paper, but imagine how interesting it would be if that pen were a Chinese calligraphy brush, and the paper made by hand! Contact your local arts center (or ask the art teacher at school) if there are calligraphy or paper-making classes held near where you live, and try your hand at these ancient Chinese arts.

Students wear traditional clothing when they learn kung fu.

TAKE KUNG FU LESSONS

For children, martial arts training has many rewards, from increased self-confidence and motivation to overall physical and mental health. It's also fun! Sign up to learn kung fu, and practice this ancient martial art developed thousands of years ago in China. Your local recreation center may be a good source for inexpensive classes, or you can check the Internet or telephone directory.

Chinese orchestra member plays a traditional instrument.

SEE A CHINESE CONCERT

Listening to the traditional music of China is an ear-opening experience! The music of China is built on a different harmonic system than most Western music. This is a result of some of the amazing musical instruments used in Chinese music, from the *pipa* (grand lute) to the *erhu* (python-skin fiddle). Traditional Chinese orchestras often tour the United States, and many performance halls offer educational programs to help listeners better understand the music.

Places to Visit

ASIAN ART MUSEUM, SAN FRANCISCO, CA
One of the largest museums in the Western world devoted exclusively to Asian art, with nearly 15,000 treasures in its collection

DETROIT INSTITUTE OF ARTS, DETROIT, MI
A strong and diverse collection with over 2,600 artifacts in its permanent Asian art collection

LOS ANGELES COUNTY MUSEUM OF ART, LOS ANGELES, CA
The art of China at this museum includes metalwork, lacquers, jades, and Buddhist art

THE CROW COLLECTION OF ASIAN ART, DALLAS, TX
The Arts of China collection focuses on the Qing Dynasty, with a great collection of carved jade

THE ART INSTITUTE OF CHICAGO, CHICAGO, IL
A rich collection of artifacts spanning nearly five millennia, from Chinese bronzes and ceramics to textiles and archaic jades

PHILADELPHIA MUSEUM OF ART, PHILADELPHIA, PA
The amazing collection of Asian art includes an original Chinese palace hall.

THE MINNEAPOLIS INSTITUTE OF THE ARTS, MINNEAPOLIS, MN
The Asian collection includes unique pieces of Chinese furniture and paintings, and an original reception hall from the Ming dynasty.

METROPOLITAN MUSEUM OF ART, NEW YORK, NY
The collection of Asian art here is among the most comprehensive in the West.

THE FREER GALLERY OF ART AND ARTHUR M. SACKLER GALLERY, WASHINGTON, D.C.
Explore more than 10,000 objects in one of the Western world's finest collections of Chinese art.

VISIT A MUSEUM'S CHINESE ART COLLECTION

One of the best ways to learn about the history of an ancient culture is through its art. From paintings to lacquerware, the beauty and depth of imperial Chinese art is amazing. Many museums, such as the Seattle Asian Art Museum (above), feature outstanding Chinese artifacts in their permanent collections.

Glossary

ACUPUNCTURE An ancient Chinese system of healing in which fine needles are inserted at specific points just under the skin to stimulate and disperse the body's flow of energy to relieve pain, or to treat a variety of different medical conditions

Acupuncturist inserts needles

ANCESTOR Someone from whom a person is descended. The worship of ancestors has been important in China since the Neolithic age.

BODHISATTVA In Mahayana Buddhism, an enlightened being; a figure of profound compassion who has already attained enlightenment but postpones his or her own hope of reaching eternal peace by helping others who seek nirvana

BRONZE An alloy of copper (usually about 90 percent) and tin, often mixed with small amounts of other metals. Since ancient times it has been the metal most commonly used in casting sculptures, because it is strong, durable, and easy to work.

BUDDHA The founder of Buddhism, born in 563 BC as Siddhartha Gautama; a prince from northern India who devoted his life to seeking enlightenment, or personal peace

BUDDHISM A major world religion based on the teachings of the Buddha. Buddhism took hold in ancient China and remains the most popular belief there.

CALLIGRAPHY A style of beautiful handwriting created by using special pens and brushes

CIVIL SERVICE A generic name for all the people employed by the government to carry out public services. Successful candidates need to pass tests called civil service examinations.

Calligraphy character

CIVILIZATION A culture; a particular society at a particular time and place

CONFUCIANISM A philosophy based on the teachings of Confucius in the sixth century BCE. Followers of Confucianism hope to establish a better overall world by means of improving each individual within their society.

CONFUCIUS The ancient Chinese philosopher and sage who lived from 551 to 479 BCE. He became China's most influential philosopher and a leading political reformer.

Great cormorant

CORMORANT A dark-colored Asian seabird that plunges into the water and snaps up fish. The cormorant stores its catch in a stretchy pouch of skin on its long neck.

CRIB Anything used to help a person cheat on an exam; for example, the handkerchief covered with civil-service-exam answers on page 19

CROSSBOW A weapon for shooting arrows, consisting of a bow placed crosswise on a wooden stock that is grooved to direct the arrow

DAOISM (or TAOISM) A system of philosophy that advocates a simple, honest life and cautions against interfering with the course of natural events

DIVINATION STICKS Special sticks used to help people foretell the future, by connecting with divine spirits

DYNASTY A succession of rulers from the same family or line; in imperial China, a succession of emperors who were usually related

ELIXIR A mythical liquid thought to grant eternal life to anyone who drinks it; sought by both Chinese and European alchemists

FERRULE A cap attached to the end of a shaft for strength or to prevent splitting

FINIAL A decorative detail used to top an object. Manchu caps were topped with finials that showed a civil servant's rank.

GUNPOWDER a mixture of chemicals (usually potassium nitrate, charcoal, and sulfur) that was once used to ignite fireworks, or as a propellant charge. Also known as black powder.

HALBERD A shafted weapon with an axlike cutting blade; similar to the Chinese quando

INKSTONE A smooth, hard, shallow tray of stone or pottery, used to mix ink sticks or cakes with water in calligraphy

IRON CASTING Using a steady blast of heat to produce a stronger form of iron; developed by the Chinese in the 6th century BCE

JADE A semiprecious gemstone, usually green but sometimes whitish, that can be worked to a high polish

JUNK A Chinese flat-bottomed sailing boat with a high stern

LACQUER A waterproof varnish made by layering several coats of treated tree sap. Colors can be combined and layered in relief as well as carved. In Chinese art, the most popular colors are red and black. Lacquer is applied to wood, bamboo, cloth, ceramics, and metals.

LONG In Chinese mythology, the name for a type of majestic dragon that dwells in rivers, lakes, and oceans and also roams the skies. Long became the symbol of the Chinese emperor.

MAGNETIC COMPASS A handheld instrument with a magnet inside which pivots freely. Because Earth is a giant magnet, the magnet in the compass will always point toward the Earth's poles, to indicate north and south.

Divination stick

NAIL GUARDS Decorative fingertip covers used to protect the long nails of the upper classes during the later years of the Chinese empire

ORACLE BONES Animal bones or shells, inscribed with writing, used to foretell the future in ancient China. One famous set contains the oldest known example of Chinese written language.

Oracle bones

MILLET A bland cereal grass that can be boiled for cereal or ground for flour

MONGOL A member of the nomadic peoples of Mongolia, in Asia. In the 12th and 13th centuries, the Mongols conquered most of Asia and Eastern Europe and ran a vast trading empire.

MOTHER-OF-PEARL The hard, smooth, iridescent inner-shell lining of oysters, mussels, and other molluks. Mother-of-pearl is milky white to silvery gray.

MOXIBUSTION Part of the traditional practice of acupuncture, involving burning the dried and crumbled leaves of an herb plant known as moxa near acupuncture points of the body

Bronze halberd

PADDY A field where rice is grown

PAGODA An Eastern temple, particularly in the form of a multistory, tapering tower, each story having its own roof

PEASANT A country person or small farmer

PHILOSOPHY The study of, or search for, knowledge, wisdom, and an understanding of the nature of the universe

PLOWSHARE In agriculture, a sharp steel wedge that cuts loose the top layer of the soil before planting

PUFU A long Chinese coat worn over other clothing

QIN Also known as Yang Qin, a stringed Chinese musical instrument resembling the Western zither

REBELLION An organized opposition to authority

SAMPAN A small Chinese boat, usually propelled by two oars

SCROLL A roll of paper which is unfurled at one end and rolled up at the other to reveal its text

SHENG A Chinese musical instrument similar to a harmonica, with 17 pipes extending upward from a metal bowl

SILK ROAD The historical trade route linking the Eastern Mediterranean basin to Central and East Asia. It got its name because of the silk, tea, and jade carried along the route from China.

SILKWORM A white caterpillar of the Chinese silkworm moth, which is the source of most commercial silk. Silkworms spin dense cocoons, each of which contains a single strand of interwoven silk.

TAOTIE A representation of a terrifying animal face with staring eyes, horns, and fangs, used on ritual objects in the Shang dynasty

Taotie

TERRACOTTA A reddish brown clay that is fired but not glazed

WOODBLOCK An ancient method of printing in which characters are carved in reverse on a wooden block. Inking the surface of the block and pressing it against a sheet of paper makes a print.

YIN AND YANG Two opposing forces in Chinese cosmology that together make up everything in the Universe. Yin is the feminine element, associated with night, and yang is the masculine element, associated with the day.

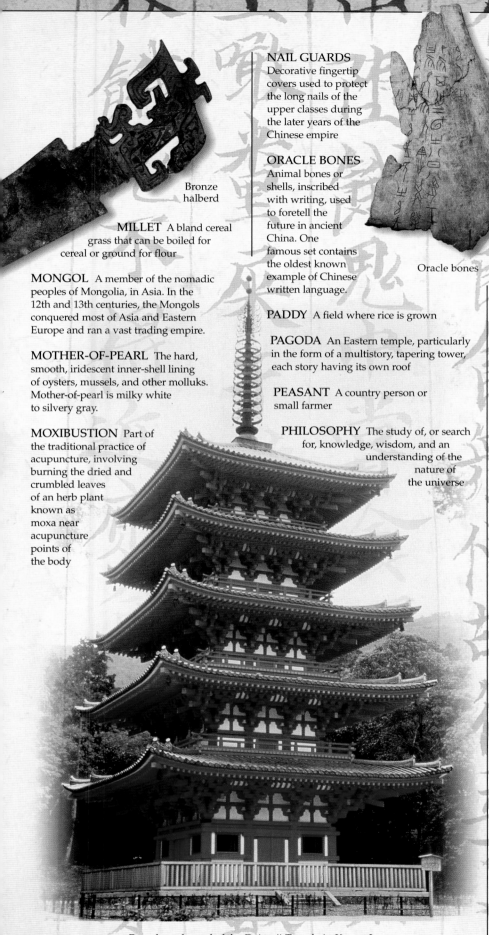

Pagoda-style roof of the Daigo-ji Temple in Kyoto, Japan

Index

Acknowledgments

The publisher would like to thank:
The staff of the Department of Oriental Antiquities at the British Museum, London, in particular Chris Kirby, Jane Newson and Christine Wilson – with special thanks to Anne Farrer; the British Museum Photographic Department, especially Ivor Kerslake; Marina de Alarçon at the Pitt Rivers Museum, Oxford; Shelagh Vainker at the Ashmolean Museum, Oxford; John Osborne at the Museum of Mankind, London; Monica Mei at the Acumedic Centre, London; the Guanghwa Company Ltd., London; Helena Spiteri for editorial help; Sharon Spencer, Susan St. Louis and Isaac Zamora for design help.

Additional photography by Peter Anderson (62cl, 63cl), Matthew Chattle (50-51l), Andy Crawford (13tr), Philip Dowell (52cl), David Gowers (59c), Chas Howson (23cr, 58bl), Ivor Kerslake (40tl), Dave King (2bl,cr, 40cl), Laurence Pordes (11cr, 19br, 24bl,cr, 25tl,bl), Ranald MacKecknie (54cl), and James Stevenson (23tl, 60-61c)
Maps by Simone End
Index by Hilary Bird

Picture credits
a=above, b=below, c=center, l=left, r=right

Bridgeman Art Library/Bibliotheque Nationale, Paris 16cr, 27tl
By permission of the British Library 24cl
©British Museum 58cl,cr
J. Allan Cash Ltd. 6br
Courtesy Chinese Cultural Embassy 16cl
Comstock/George Gerster 16br, 35tl
Arthur Cotterell 15cl, 22c, 23tr, 24tc, 31cl, 32tr, 44tl,cl, 50br, 53cr, 55tl, 58tl, 62tl
R.V. Dunning FC tl,br, 18c,bc, 31tl, 41bc
ET Archive 34tl;/Bibliotheque Nationale, Paris 18tl,39tl,54tl;/British Museum FC bl, BC tc, 20tl, 38tl;/Freer Gallery of Art 35cr,

36cr;/National Palace Museum, Taiwan 42bl;/Private Collection 62b;/Courtesy Trustees Victoria & Albert Museum 50cr, 57cr
Mary Evans Picture Library 8tr, 12tl, 59tr;/T'Ongjen Tschen Kierou King 28bl;/Petit Journal BC br, 63tl, Vittorio Pisari in La Tribuna Illustrata 63br
Robert Harding Picture Library 16tr;/Collection of the National Palace Museum,/Taipei, Taiwan, Republic of China 59bl
Mansell Collection 26tr, 36tl
National Maritime Museum 63bl
The Needham Research Institute 16bl, 22br
The Nelson-Atkins Museum of Art, Kansas City, Missouri (Purchase: Nelson Trust) 33-1559, 33tr
Photographie Giraudon 40bl
Photostage/Donald Cooper 52tl
Roger-Viollet 60bl
©Science Museum 22bl
Courtesy Trustees of Victoria & Albert

Museum 46br, 54cl;/Ian Thomas BC tl, 16clb, 21t,bc, 54-5b, 63tr
Alamy: Panorama Stock Photos Co Ltd 65cl, 66tl; Helge Pedersen 68bl; Chuck Pefley 68cr
Corbis: 67br; Asian Art & Archaeology, Inc. 66bl; Dean Conger 65tr; Werner Forman 70br; Walter Hodges 69tl; Gunter Marx Photography 69bc; Royal Ontario Museum 66-67tc, 71tr; Sakamoto Photo Research Laboratory 71bl
Getty Images: National Geographic 65bl
The Granger Collection, New York: 71br

Jacket images: *Front:* Alamy Images: View Stock (cb). DK Images: Alan Hills/The British Museum (cal, tl); Geoff Brightling/ Pitt Rivers Museum, University of Oxford (tr); Geoff Brightling/The British Museum (cla). *Back:* DK Images: Alan Hills/The British Museum (bl, cfr); James Stevenson and Tina Chambers/National Maritime Museum, London (br).